DMS ColourScene Volume Three

N. J. Eadon-Clarke

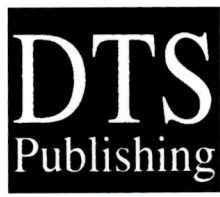

DTS Publishing

First published 2004
ISBN: 1 900515 90 3
Published by DTS, PO Box 105, Croydon, UK
Printed by Unwin Brothers, Old Woking
© N. J. Eadon-Clarke 2004

British Library Cataloguing in Publication Data. A catalogue record for this book is available from the British Library.

All rights reserved. Except for normal review purposes no part of this book may be reproduced or utilised in any form or by any means, electrical or mechanical, including photocopying, recording or by an information storage and retrieval system, without the prior written consent of DTS Publishing, PO Box 105, Croydon, CR9 2TL

DTS Publishing www.BooksDTS.co.uk

ABOVE: A mounted policeman and London taxicab pass Ensignbus / London Pride DMS 188 near Charing Cross Railway Station in the Strand. The black livery for Kronenbourg lager ensures the vehicle stands out from the crowd. **28 September 1986**

FRONT COVER: Warrington Borough Transport acquired their six DMSs in late 1980, and they entered service progressively between Nov 80 and Jun 81. Two are seen here in Buttermarket Street. DMS 1487 is now Warrington 95 and DMS 1503 is now Warrington 98. DMS 1487 was destined to be the last DMS in the Warrington fleet lasting until 1992. **13 July 1985**

FRONTISPIECE: 3211: Only two DMSs with Cumberland Motor Services had received the new fleet livery at the time of my visit. One that had was DMS 2170 seen here looking extremely smart with DMS 2169 and DMS 2224 in the background in Carlisle city centre. Later in 1988 the entire batch of ten would move together again to Fareway of Kirkby, Merseyside. **14 April 1988**

Contents

Section 1	USA – Denver and Chicago – 1991	4
Section 2	UK – 1985	10
Section 3	Hong Kong – 1981-1995	21
Section 4	UK – 1986	30
Section 5	China – Guangzhou – 1993-1994	52
Section 6	UK – 1987	56
Section 7	USA – New York – 1994	72
Section 8	UK – 1988	76
Section 9	China – Jilin and Dalian – 1997-2001	101

All photographs by the Author unless otherwise stated

DMS ColourScene
Volume Three
Foreword

This book continues the story started in DMS ColourScene 1979 – 1984 and DMS ColourScene Hong Kong. With the exception of the photographs taken in Dalian and Jilin and a few in Hong Kong, it contains my personal photographs of LT DMS type Daimler Fleetlines after sale by London Transport.

The UK photographs start in 1985 and continue until 1988; in order to provide more variety it also covers my initial visits to USA to show examples in Denver, Chicago and New York.

The Hong Kong and Guangzhou photographs cover the period 1981 to 1995. I am indebted to Lennox MacEwan for providing the photographs in Dalian and Jilin and also for his help prior to my visits to Guangzhou. I am unaware of any other photographs of double deckers in Jilin and his annual visits to Dalian allow a comprehensive pictorial record of the Tong DA Bus Company fleet.

I must also express my thanks to Mike Davis of DTS Publishing for providing some of his Hong Kong photos and for putting this book together and the advice provided at all stages of production and also to Maurice Bateman for information on Denver, Chicago and New York.

I acknowledge the help given by the many owners and operators of vehicles depicted in this book. Particular thanks are due to Peter Newman of Ensignbus who allowed frequent visits to his Purfleet site and was always willing to answer various questions.

Finally I am grateful to Keith Hamer for the regular supply of information on former London vehicles and his book titled 'Where have all the DMSs gone' proved a valuable source of reference. Information was also taken from and shared with The London Omnibus Traction Society and the PSV Circle over the years from 1979.

These photographs illustrate the colourful lives of the class around the world after disposal by London Transport; I hope you find this collection of photographs enjoyable and a reminder that the DMS proved a valuable workhorse to operators large and small.

Copies of both DMS ColourScene 1979 – 1984 and DMS ColourScene Hong Kong are still available. Contact the publisher at the address shown above or via their web page for price information.

Nigel Eadon-Clarke
Chislehurst
Kent
UK

July 2004

BELOW: DMS 2069 is now numbered 5027 in the Maidstone & District fleet; seen here approaching the entrance ramp leading to the Pentagon Shopping Centre bus station. Note the limited blind display and white grill housing the attack alarm. **25 May 1985**

USA – Denver 1991

ABOVE: British Double Decker of Denver, USA acquired 10 early DMSs in 1983. In 1991 seven examples remained operational and here all seven stand outside their garage specially lined up for these and subsequent photographs by Ed Crawley the garage manager. From left to right are former DMSs 185, 232, 180, 147, 304, 283 & 363. **14 October 1991**

RIGHT: One of the three non operational DMSs with British Double Decker is former DMS 340 seen here behind their garage. This bus carries local fleet number BDD 009 in the rear registration box. This bus had slight front end damage when this photograph was taken. **14 October 1991**

FAR RIGHT: The front of former DMS 211 now British Double Decker BDD 004, taken from outside their yard through the fence. From this view it can be seen that the bus is named *Liverpool* and judging from the faded paint and missing windows has not been used for a considerable time. **14 October 1991**

RIGHT: Offside view of *Big Ben*, former DMS 363 at the Denver garage yard. **14 October 1991**

4

RIGHT: The remains of ex-T DMS 312 in the rear yard of the "British Double-Decker", Denver, Colorado. Also in the picture is the rear of another ex-London bus, T 3173 and a Bristol VR, CS 971C – actually WY977G. **14 October 1991**

CENTRE RIGHT 3303: Offside view of *Baker St* former DMS 304 standing with DMS 283 and DMS 363 in the Denver yard. **14 October 1991**

BELOW: British Double Decker, BDD 005 is named *Chelsea*; it is former DMS 232. DMS 185, *Trafalgar*, is behind. **14 October 1991**

5

USA – Chicago 1991

RIGHT: Between 1986 and 1991 Chicago Motor Coach Company received a total of 17 DMs amongst many other British Buses. Here CMCC 528 the former DM 1710 stands in Superior Street, Chicago. The centre exit door has been transferred to the opposite side to allow loading in American streets, compare this with the photograph later in this book. **20 October 1991**

BELOW: The rear of CMCC 528 former DM 1710 standing in Superior Street Chicago showing the full depth rear advertisement. **20 October 1991**

BELOW RIGHT: Inside the Chicago Motor Coach Company garage at 750 South Clinton sees former DM 1101 which was damaged during delivery and in consequence was used as a source of spare parts despite being given the CMCC fleet number of 552 a number later reassigned to former DMS 1949 when that was rebuilt. **21 October 1991**

BOTTOM LEFT: This is former DMS 1949 parked in the corner of the Chicago parking yard of CMCC showing some signs of roof damage. This was allocated the fleet number 553 on paper, but by the time it was refurbished and entered service it took fleet number 552 originally intended to be DM 1101, see previous photo. **21 October 1991**

BOTTOM RIGHT: Also received from Ensignbus earlier in 1991 was former DM 926 seen at the parking yard of CMCC awaiting attention. This bus was allocated fleet number 554 for use in Chicago. **21 October 1991**

RIGHT: This is the unique LHD former DMS 729 which had been exported to Chicago Motor Coach in January 1986 and numbered 513. It is parked out of use in their parking area with false number plate BCS969C. If you look carefully you can see that the front door has been removed and replaced by the drivers cab. Sadly this bus would not re-enter service with CMCC before being scrapped. **1 October 1991**

BELOW: This bus had been in service in Chicago for five years by the time this photograph was taken in Superior Street. The vehicle is former DM 1037 now numbered 516 in the CMCC fleet. **22 October 1991**

RIGHT: Inside the garage of Chicago Motor Coach Company at 750 South Clinton showing the restricted headroom. On the far side is CMCC 528 former DM 1710. In the centre is CMCC 547 former fleetline FJA206D and nearest the camera is CMCC 521 a replica 'B' type mounted on a Mercedes Benz L508D LHD chassis. **22 October 1991**

7

LEFT: Two former London buses meet outside the Sears Tower in Chicago. On the left is CMCC 542 former LCBS AN 100 carrying bogus registration NAC417F, it is being passed by former DM 1037 now CMCC 516. **23 October 1991**

CENTRE: The bridge is up across the Chicago river behind CMCC Nos. 514 and 516 at the Wacker Drive stop. These buses are former DMS 1701 and DM 1037 respectively. **23 October 1991**

BOTTOM: This is former DM 1157 now CMCC 525 seen leaving the Wacker Drive stop in Chicago with the bridge over the Chicago river seen raised behind. This bus was also pictured with Ebdon's in 'DMS ColourScene 1979 – 1984'. **23 October 1991**

LEFT: Chicago Motor Coach No.526 was originally DM1072 and one of several former Ebdons vehicles to migrate to Chicago, the repositioned centre doors can be seen clearly which are necessary for American streets. **21 October 1991**

LEFT: Another former Ebdons vehicle is DM 1113 now Chicago Motor Coach No. 523 seen in the parking yard at Roosevelt/Jefferson two blocks south of the main garage. **21 October 1991**

BELOW: Chicago Motor Coach parking yard with the Sears Tower in the background. On the left is DM 939 now CMCC 515 and on the right is the rear of RM 2017. To some, however, the most unusual vehicle in this view is the ex-Vienna bus with Gräff & Stift bodywork on an M.A.N chassis. **21 October 1991**

9

United Kingdom – 1985

TOP LEFT: Former DMS 290 prepares to leave London County Hall in its new role as the Islington Crèche and Information bus. This bus would later pass to Stirling District Council for continued use as a playbus. **9 March 1985**

TOP RIGHT: DMS 1682 was repainted by its new operator Ensignbus into '1933' livery during 1983, two years later is seen passing St. Pauls Cathedral on the Round London Sightseeing Tour still carrying that livery. **21 April 1985**

ABOVE: Also passing St Pauls Cathedral is DMS 589 now numbered CB4, in the Culturebus fleet, notice the addition of red and orange bands since pictured in DMS ColourScene 1979-1984. **21 April 1985**

LEFT: A pair of Ebdons vehicles seek trade outside the British Airways office in London's Regent Street. DM 1021 seen here would have several subsequent owners before returning again to London Sightseeing work with Big Bus. **6 May 1985**

10

ABOVE: London Pride Sightseeing set up a London Sightseeing service to compete with London Transport and adopted a unique livery as far removed from plain LT red as is possible to imagine. DM 1069 stands outside the Trocadero in London. This vehicle was later to become something of a favorite with Ensignbus and still exists with a private owner in 2004 although in store, following several years use at Whipsnade Zoo. **6 May 1985**

ABOVE RIGHT: The Mayhew group based in Uckfield acquired DMS 1604 to transport their employees to their homes between Uckfield and Eastbourne. It is seen here specifically posed for the writer on Eastbourne sea front. The logo represents a chicken; the processing of which is the Company's main activity. **12 May 1985**

RIGHT: Nelson Independent Bus Services of Wickford Essex would eventually operate six DMSs in their fleet. DM 1803 seen here outside their garage was the first to be acquired, note the retention of the centre exit door. **19 May 1985**

RIGHT: The next two vehicles acquired by Nelson Independent Bus Services were DM 1721 & DM 1797. They were operated initially in as acquired LT red livery, but a start has been made in repainting DM1721. They are both seen here posed for the writer outside their garage in Wickford. **19 May 1985**

11

ABOVE LEFT: Due to the proximity of Southend Transport with Ensignbus it is not surprising that a close working relationship would exist. Southend Transport carried out vehicle preparation work for Ensignbus and from 1984 onwards operated a variety of DMSs on long term loan from Ensignbus. Here we see DMS 1949 in the Central Bus Station, note the 'No Change Given' notice on the front panel and the Eastern National VR behind. **24 May 1985**

ABOVE RIGHT: Another DM in the Southend Transport fleet was DM 1106 it collects passengers in the central bus station. Notice the unusually positioned fleetnumber (313) behind the drivers cab window. **24 May 1985**

LEFT: DM1830 in the yard of Waterhouse Coaches at Polegate showing how smart a DMS can look in white, the route number box proclaims the bus or company as No.1. **1 June 1985**

LEFT: The Harlow Majorettes acquired DMS 1449 to transport their troupe to events. The livery appears to be based on a Stars and Stripes theme. It stands here outside Thurrock Civic Centre. **2 June 1985**

TOP LEFT: OK Motor Services of Bishop Auckland acquired several DMSs in a dealer capacity. The only one to pass into their associated fleet of Lockeys was DMS 1258 seen here at the OK garage in the unusual black and cream livery with a former LT Bristol LH visible behind. Notice also the early form of centre door removal with a square window and the deflector mounted on the front panel designed to keep the wing mirror free of dirt. **8 June 1985**

TOP RIGHT: Tricolour coaches of Newgate Street Village operated one double decker. Despite the fleetname the livery was plain white. DM 1715 was the vehicle in question seen here at their base in company with a rare Caetano bodied coach. **16 June 1985**

ABOVE LEFT: South Midland Ltd commenced operation of open top sightseeing tours in Oxford in 1985. Existing open top vehicles were acquired from the Ensignbus sightseeing operations. One of the two initial vehicles was DM 1121 seen in relatively empty Oxford on the tour to Blenheim Palace and Woodstock. **2 June 1985**

ABOVE RIGHT: The second South Midland vehicle was DMS 886 which carried a light brown and cream livery for a circular tour of Oxford. Numbered T1 it stands in Oxford city centre. **2 June 1985**

RIGHT: DM 1245 was acquired by British Telecom and converted into a mobile phoneshop for use at summer fetes and other special events. It is seen here at the Little Milton village fete in its original livery. **22 June 1985**

13

ABOVE LEFT: Thamesdown Transport Ltd of Swindon were never slow to pick up a bargain, hence their acquisition of a dozen DMSs in 1983/4. DMS 2239 displays the original livery on a sunny summer's day in Fleming Way. **6 July 1985**

ABOVE RIGHT: Ensignbus renumbered DMS 343 to DMO 343 following its open top conversion. It is seen parked at Marble Arch. **6 July 1985**

LEFT: DMS 36 was a somewhat elusive vehicle in the dealer fleet of E H Brakell. In this view it is parked in Pall Mall while on loan to London Pride to provide cover in the event of a failure of another bus. **6 July 1985**

BELOW: The first DMS to enter service with Warrington was DMS 1504 seen here in Buttermarket Street. Note the revised front indicators and the painted adverts. **13 July 1985**

RIGHT: Standing in the Chadwell Heath yard of Pathfinder we find DM 1051 which had recently been acquired from Southern Star Coaches of Harlow. This would subsequently pass to Shoreys of Maulden and still exists in 2004 being preserved by a private owner. **3 August 1985**

LEFT: Ensignbus DMO 264 the former DMS 264 stands in the yard of LT's Chiswick works during an open day. The neat open top conversion by Ensignbus deserves credit. **11 August 1985**

RIGHT: In DMS ColourScene 1979-1984, I illustrated the first Ensign Enterprise conversion (DMS 2148). By 1985 its livery had changed to that shown here when it was parked behind the second conversion, DMS 90 (A741 TTW,) on the Embankment for the lunch break. **12 August 1985**

15

ABOVE LEFT: DMS 2000 initially operated for Trathens Travel Services Ltd a company linked with Culturebus in a blue livery for Trafalgar Tours. Early in 1985 it was repainted into this livery as a standby vehicle for the main Culturebus fleet numbered CB7 and named 'Mr Bumble'. It is seen here in Kingsway about to turn into the Aldwych. **13 August 1985**

ABOVE RIGHT: Shorey's Travel 'Colley Sampson Mover' DMS 1893 was the first DMS to be registered with a cherished plate (DDA66). It stands in their Maulden yard with their other DMS1849 visible behind. Shorey's DMSs all received painted all over adverts for most of their lives with the operator. **17 August 1985**

LEFT: Buffalo Travel of Flitwick operated various DMSs in their fleet from 198? until their take over by Dunn Line in 2002. Most vehicles carried a red livery, but the very first DM 1706 carried this eye catching scheme. It was specially posed for the camera in their yard. **17 August 1985**

LEFT: Another unusual livery illustrated by DMS 1728 in the yard of its new owner, Ronsway of Hemel Hempstead. **17 August 1985**

RIGHT: Simmonds Coaches of Letchworth operated the two DMSs seen here (DMS 989 acquired in 9/83 and DMS 1948 acquired in 8/84) DMS 1948 operated in LT red livery until mid 1986. The owner told me that these two vehicles were as different as 'chalk and cheese' in their driving characteristics. **August 1985**

ABOVE: Borough of Barrow-in-Furness Corporation Transport obtained 5 DMSs in 1983/4. All five would pass to Chester City Transport in 1988. Here DMS 2227 shows the initial livery and limited destination blind display outside the garage of its new owner. **24 August 1985**

ABOVE RIGHT: In Barrow-in-Furness town centre DMS 2174 now Barrow 101 awaits custom. This bus still exists and acts as a clubroom with a gliding club in Denbigh North Wales. **24 August 1985**

RIGHT: Barrow 108 DMS 2041 loads up in Barrow-in-Furness. **24 August 1985**

17

ABOVE: The third Ensign Enterprise conversion was numerically the oldest vehicle, DMS 237 was re-registered B56DAR such was the amount of change during its conversion. Seen here on the Victoria Embankment just a few months after completion in front of the second conversion DMS 590 re-registered A741TTW. **2 September 198**

ABOVE RIGHT: Nearside view of Ensign Enterprise A741TTW (DMS 590) while parked on the Embankment showing the plug type door conversion. **2 September 198**

BELOW LEFT: Bedlington & District Luxury Coaches moved to new premises in Ashington and very smartly painted DMS 559 stands next to others in their ne yard. **7 September 1985**

BELOW RIGHT: DMS 1263 was one of the first two DMSs acquired by Bedlington in 1979. Seen here in their new yard still looking in very good condition despite being worke hard over poor road surfaces for the preceding 6 years. **7 September 1985**

BOTTOM: Park Royal bodied DMS 416 stands next to MCW bodied DMSs 1468 and 1298 in the new yard of Bedlington and District. DMS 416 would be only DMS from th fleet to see further use after withdrawal by Bedlington. It remains extant in 2004 with a car dealership in Perth Scotland. **7 September 1985**

ABOVE: DM 1220 was unique as the only DMS to be modified after sale by [N]BT to be fitted with a removable roof. Unlike other DMSs in the South Wales fleet it carried Skyrider livery. The rings in the roof to facilitate its removal can clearly be seen in this view in Swansea bus station. It is doubtful whether it ever actually operated in open top form. **14 September 1985**

ABOVE RIGHT: Representative of the DMSs in the South Wales fleet is DMS 1924 seen in Swansea bus station on a wet September day. **14 September 1985**

RIGHT: DM 1237 now South Wales 851 numerically the first in their fleet reverses off the stand in Swansea bus station. One year later on withdrawal this bus together with DMS2011 would be the first ex NBC DMSs to pass to independents in this case to Coaches of Swansea. **14 September 1985**

RIGHT: The weather has improved and DMS 1924 backs off the stand at Swansea bus station amongst various Leyland Nationals. **14 September 1985**

19

TOP LEFT: An unexpected surprise during my visit Swansea was the appearance of DM 1802 one of fo DMSs acquired the previous month by D Coaches. carries advertising for Morriston Travel Centre anoth business in the same group. **14 September 1985**

TOP RIGHT: DMS 1283 was illustrated in DM ColourScene 1979-1984. Some four years later its front appearance has been transformed by the fitting of a ne Roe style roof front dome and vents beside the blin boxes. It was moved out of the garage for this photograp to be taken during a depot visit by the M&D and Ea Kent Bus Club. **28 September 1985**

ABOVE LEFT: Also illustrated in DMS ColourScen 1979-1984 was DMS 1552 in the ownership of C Coaches of Cardiff. Subsequently the bus passed Stevensons before joining the Astill & Jordan of Ratb fleet. Seen here in Leicester freshly out of the paint sho and still awaiting the application of adverts on their rou 94 to Ratby. **28 September 1985**

ABOVE RIGHT: DMS 136 as seen here was kept for time in a corner of the yard at Slough garage when n in active use. It was owned by World Educatio Berkshire as a promotional vehicle and later passed the Dyfed Fire & Rescue Service. **6 October 1985**

LEFT: A site familiar to London Bus enthusiasts Hounslow bus station. Here we find DM 1019 owned b London Buslines who had won the contract for route 8 three months earlier. This was the first tendered L route to be operated with DMSs. Note the notice carrie on the front to advise intending passengers that despi the livery this was still a LRT route on which passe would be accepted. **6 October 1985**

Hong Kong 1981–1995

LEFT: Although China Motor Bus had been the first Hong Kong operator to introduce the ex-London DMS-class, Chung Wah Shipbuilding and Engineering were the first non-franchised (independent) operator in the former Colony to use DMSs and took three, ex-DMS626, 606 and 663 which were registered in Hong Kong in January, March and April 1981 respectively as Chung Wah Nos 1, 2 and 3. Prior to shipping, Ensign removed the centre exit doorway and half the front doorway and, at the same time, increased seating to 105 by using the 2+3 arrangement, with five rearward facing seats across the upper-deck front. Hong Kong vehicle examiners frowned upon such a high capacity with only a narrow front doorway in case of emergency and required that the full-width doorway be reinstated and seating reduced to 100. Here Chung Wah No3 ex-DMS 663 awaits the attention of the bodybuilder for that purpose at rival Citybus premises. **13 March 1981.** *(Mike Davis)*

LEFT: In 1982, Citybus obtained a contract to run an open-top bus tour and arranged for Ensign to ship a late model DMS already converted for the purpose. This arrived in the form of ex-DMS2150 and was painted into a colourful livery loosely based on that carried by a Scania demonstrator of the period and numbered D23. Unfortunately, before the painting was completed, the contract fell through and D23 remained unlicensed, being used for Citybus promotional work until August 1983. It was photographed here, running on trade plates at Kowloon Tong. **14 April 1983.** *(Mike Davis)*

LEFT: DMS2150 was eventually painted into the striking black and white livery of a Citybus associated company, Vanguard Transport for London-style hop-on-hop-off tours. Here it is in its new livery, complete with tour guides, posed for promotional photographs at "Star" Ferry Pier. **. . 1984.** *(Mike Davis)*

21

ABOVE LEFT: Straight off the boat; D 1759 had been parked at the Hung Ho dockyard that served as the Citybu depot in the early 1980's before havin its centre doorway removed and i seating increased to 100, using the 3+ arrangement on the upper deck. Th was to become Citybus L18. **July 198** *(Mike Davis)*

ABOVE: Citybus L12 painted as a pil to demonstrate the future MTR livery f a contract that was not approved by Hon Kong Government. Buses in MTR live wore Citybus labels on the waist panel Here the former DMS 788 shows the 10 seat arrangement minus center doorwa **February 1983** *(Mike Davis)*

LEFT: Again, just delivered. Th offside rear of DM 1085 at Hung Ho before becoming Citybus L19. **Ju 1981** *(Mike Davis)*

BELOW: A line-up of Fleetline between duties at the Ocean Par Nearest the camera is L19 (DM 1085 then L20 (DM1084), L15 (DMS 796 and L14 (DMS 798) and, finally, tw ex-Bournemouth Fleetlines, D4 (whi roof ex-CRU 191C) and D1 (yello roof ex-CRU 181C). **September 198** *(Mike Davis)*

RIGHT: With the CMB multi storey Chai Wan bus garage in the background DMS 916 (XF 12) is behind DMS 479 (XF 58) in the bus station. Note the additional window fitted behind the entrance door on DMS 916 whereas the rear part of the door on DMS 479 is merely bolted shut. **9 November 1990**

BELOW: DMS 240 had been used by the Chiswick Works experimental department for door experiments. It stands in Chai Wan bus station with CMB as XF 20 carrying blinds for route 104 which would use the Cross Harbour Tunnel to reach Kowloon. **9 November 1990**

ABOVE: A large new shopping centre named Pacific Place was built at Admiralty on Hong Kong Island. Standing outside the main entrance is DM 992 now CMB XF 142 carrying an all over advertisement for ESSO. **10 November 1990**

LEFT: Also outside Pacific Place is DM 1187 now XF 178 in the China Motor Bus fleet carrying an all over advertisement for JCB, not earth moving equipment, but a bank card. **10 November 1990**

LEFT: DMS 2092 was one of th[e] last batch of DMSs exported to Hon[g] Kong, it became CMB XF 201 an[d] pauses outside Pacific Plac[e] shopping centre at Admiralt[y]. **10 November 1990**

CENTRE LEFT: Also at Pacific Plac[e] we see an ornate livery bein[g] carried by CMB XF 169, DM 119[?]. **10 November 1990**

BELOW: The bus station at Nor[th] Point ferry on Hong Kong Island see[s] DM 983 now CMB XF 143 in th[e] bright yellow livery for café d[e] Colombia. Route 10 was a ma[in] trunk route along the northern edg[e] of the Island. **15 November 1990**

BOTTOM: Citybus No.5 DM 108[?] drops off passengers at the Sta[r] Ferry will working on the free shutt[le] service to and from the Peak Tra[m] lower terminal. **24 April 1992**

24

ABOVE: CMB route 6 was the main stopping service to Stanley village on the south side of Hong Kong Island and would travel via Happy Valley giving stunning views of the Racecourse. XF 118 was DMS 894 seen here in Connaught Road Central with rebuilt upper front. **26 April 1992**

LEFT: Rear view of CMB Training Bus T 19, DMS 557 seen in Central outside the Hilton Hotel which has since been demolished. **28 April 1992**

BELOW LEFT: The vehicles belonging to the KMB training fleet adopted this new livery by 1992. DMS 794 stands on the roof of Sha Tin garage. This bus was illustrated in the original red and yellow livery in DMS ColourScene Hong Kong. **28 April 1992**

BELOW: The sun is setting and KMB training bus DMS 1554 has just returned to its base, the roof of KMB Sha Tin garage. The driver is practicing low speed parking manoeuvres, hence the red cone indicating which parking bay should be used. **28 April 1992**

LEFT: Illustrating the old and new livery on the KMB training fleet. On the left in the new livery is DMS 1554 and on the right is DMS 1557 in the old livery. They are parked on the roof of Sha Tin garage. **28 April 1992**

CENTRE LEFT: Numerous ex-London buses in the yard of Argos Bus Services on the island of Tsing Yi carrying the new grey livery. Argos 21 is DMS 184 looking the worse for wear and Argos 36 is MD 66. Just visible behind is Argos 73, DMS 2145 which was acquired from Citybus in September 1990 it had been D26 in the fleet. **30 April 1992**

BELOW LEFT: Just arrived at Stanley village on the south side of Hong Kong Island is DMS 902 now XF 141 in the CMB fleet. **1 May 1992**

BELOW: Demonstrating the method of altering the destination blind display is CMB XF 160 at Stanley Village, this bus is DM 1053. **1 May 1992**

RIGHT: One of the earliest numerically DMSs exported to Hong Kong was DMS 167. It was first licensed in Hong Kong in March 1981. Eleven years later it was still going strong and had thus operated longer in Hong Kong than it had in London. It is seen at Admiralty in a livery for Sanyo. **2 May 1992**

BELOW: Yau Fong Tours acquired DMS 2160 from Citybus. The livery was very similar to that used by Stagecoach which caused some conflict when Stagecoach started their own operations in Hong Kong. It is seen near their yard in Sha Tin. **2 May 1992**

ABOVE: Citybus No. 6 was DMS 2144. It is parked at Admiralty between duties. **3 May 1992**

LEFT: The Kennedy Town terminus showing vehicles parked on the pavement between the rush hours. On the left is CMB XF 128, DMS 911 and next to it is XF 132 DMS 929. **3 May 1992**

LEFT: DMS 638 has become CMB XF 46: it takes on passengers at Pacific Place, behind is a short Dennis Dominator used on route 1 to the Peak. **9 May 1992**

RIGHT 3374: Also at Pacific Place we find CMB XF 44, DMS 316. Behind is an air conditioned Dennis from the KMB fleet on a cross harbour service. **9 May 1992**

LEFT: DMS 891 in an all over advertisement livery for Daiwa Bank operating for the China Motor Bus company as their XF 125 pauses outside Pacific Place at Admiralty. **9 May 1992**

28

FAR LEFT: In the corner of the yard of Speedybus at Ping Che in the far north of the New Territories is DMS 2426 which is kept in preserved condition. **27 April 1994**

LEFT: This is believed to be DMS 605 in use as a storeroom outside the Speedybus yard at Ping Che. This bus was pictured in use with the KMB training fleet whose livery it still carries in DMS ColourScene Hong Kong. **27 April 1994**

LEFT: DMS 2466 was fitted with an experimental Ashok engine while in the UK. It was subsequently purchased by Speedybus and is seen here tucked away in their yard at Ping Che. **11 November 1995**

FAR LEFT CENTRE: Badly damaged DMS 2374 stands in the yard of Speedybus at Ping Che. **11 November 1995**

LEFT: An obscure scrapyard in Ping Che Road New Territories sees DMS 765 previously in the KMB training fleet in the process of being scrapped. **11 November 1995**

BELOW: Shortly after China Motor Bus lost a further number of routes to Citybus in 1995, large quantities of buses were withdrawn overnight and driven to this remote site [in] Yuen Long near the China mainland border. Partly obscured by earth moving equipment, they were also protected by free roaming dogs, on the extreme right is DM 927 [a]nd next to it DMS 835. **11 November 1995**

United Kingdom – 1986

ABOVE LEFT: Limebourne Coaches trading as Cityrama were a well established London Sightseeing company when they successfully tendered to operate route 200 from March 1986. Further DMSs were acquired to operate this route including DM 1831 seen here in Streatham H with Brixton garage behind **27 March 1986**

ABOVE: In Spring 1986 there was a by election in Fulham. For several weeks prior to election day the Labour Party used their DMS 2023 for promotion and publicity purposes. Rear offside view of DMS 2023 owned by the Labour Party seen in Fulham Road **5 April 1986**

LEFT: The open rear top deck allowed the candidate (in this case Nic Raynsford) to broadcast his policies on the move. Seen here near the local Labour Party office in Fulham Road before repainting to reflect the revised livery of New Labour. **5 April 1986**

LEFT: DM 958 was another of the DMSs acquired by Limebourne Coaches Ltd to operate LRT route 200, it stands at the new Brixton terminus, the previous terminus of route 200 had been Brixton garage which was no longer appropriate once the route passed to an independent operator. **5 April 1986**

LEFT: Frog Island Fish farm at Abinger Hammer is the location of DMS 1843 now in the ownership of David Cullen & Mister David's Associates Ltd used as a mobile hospitality and catering unit. Note how the simple re-positioning of the front number plate changes the frontal appearance. **13 April 1986**

LEFT: Earlier in this book we saw Ensignbus DMS 1682 in '1933' Sightseeing livery. One year later it has received standard Ensignbus fleet livery although still used on London Pride Sightseeing tours. It takes a break in the car park behind the old Crawley bus station en route for a day trip to Brighton on the day of the annual HCVC London to Brighton run. **4 May 1986**

BELOW LEFT: DM 1001 only operated for Horsham Coaches of Warnham for eighteen months, nevertheless it carried an attractive paint scheme as seen in their yard only spoilt by the blank destination screens. **4 May 1986**

BELOW: Davian Coaches of Enfield operated three DMSs. Here we see DMS 2216 in their yard which also contains ex East Kent Regent V WFN 831. **10 May 1986**

31

RIGHT: DMS 2221 pauses for the photographer in the yard of Davian Coaches at Enfield, note that this operator decided to retain the centre exit doors. **10 May 1986**

CENTRE LEFT and RIGHT: Following their experience with the production of the three Ensign Enterprise conversions for 'The Londoners' pictured earlier in this book Ensignbus used their knowledge to produce a high specification hospitality bus for their own use. The vehicle selected was DMS 852 and it is seen here outside their workshop carrying the cherished number plate 31 DOO. If you look carefully you can just make out 'Swan Lager' on the front panel above the windscreen; this had been applied when the vehicle was used to transport the England Test Cricket Team who was sponsored by the makers of Swan Lager. **The righthand picture** shows the rear view of DMS 852 outside the Ensignbus workshops showing the rear end treatment. **Both 18 May 1986**

RIGHT: A prospective sale to Mecca saw large numbers of DMSs being painted cream and prepared for export. In the event the sale fell through because the purchaser would not provide the money before the buses were shipped. Most buses were diverted to other buyers. DM1132 would pass to London Sightseeing Tours and subsequently to New York. DMS 2167 and DMS 1898 would pass to Metrobus to operate LRT routes 61 and 361. **18 May 1986**

ABOVE: In *'DMS ColourScene 1979 -1984'*, we saw DM 1758 in its original form. Here it is again outside the Ensignbus workshop in shortened form following an apprentices exercise. Apparently it was rather unstable and spent the rest of its life as a store shed at Purfleet. **18 May 1986**

RIGHT: DM 1074 being prepared for service at Purfleet. It would enter service in their own fleet the following month on LRT route 145 numbered 212. **18 May 1986**

RIGHT: One of the early DMSs that would not see further use other than by donating parts to others was DMS 24 seen here at Ensignbus awaiting final scrapping. **18 May 1986**

BELOW LEFT: DM 1134 and DM 1129 would remain parked at Purfleet providing parts for another four years before scrapping in 1990. **18 May 1986**

BELOW RIGHT: Note the headlights mounted on the centre panel of these two early DMSs parked at Purfleet. On the left is DMS 112 and next to it is DMS 64 both were ultimately scrapped. **18 May 1986**

33

ABOVE: DM 964 with roof panels removed was a vehicle destined to Mecca before the deal was cancelled; its roof would be restored to allow it to re-enter normal service as part of the Ensignbus fleet. DM 1154 and DM 1166 would also join the Ensignbus fleet. **18 May 1986**

ABOVE: Ensign stock at Purfleet included DMS 867 which would later pass to London Sightseeing Tours and early DMS 158 which would operate in the Ensignbus sightseeing fleet. DMS 158 still exists and continues on Sightseeing tours in the Canadian city of Toronto. **18 May 1986**

ABOVE RIGHT: DMS 1923 had also been destined for Mecca, hence the removal of the roof panels. Instead it would become a promotional vehicle for the Hollywood Night Club with an open rear upper deck area in similar style to that carried by DMS 2023 pictured earlier in this book. **18 May 1986**

RIGHT: More vehicles from the aborted Mecca order. Standing in the Purfleet yard are DM 1059, DM 939, DM 1170, DMS 287 and DMS 853. These would all see future service. **18 May 1986**

34

LEFT: Illustrating the Culture Bus livery following the take over of the tour by Ensignbus is DM 1738, now C204, it stands outside their workshop at Purfleet for minor body panel repair. **18 May 1986**

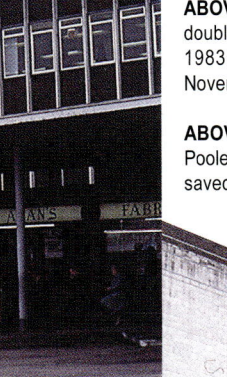

ABOVE LEFT: Wilts and Dorset took thirty DMSs to cater for an increased need for double deckers. DMS 1951 became Wilts & Dorset 1935 when it entered the fleet in 1983, it was typical of the fleet and operated until passing to the scrapyard in November 1990. It stands in Poole bus station. **23 May 1986**

ABOVE: DM 1240 became 1934 in the Wilts & Dorset fleet seen here approaching Poole bus station. Despite passing to a scrap dealer in 1990 it would be subsequently saved for further operation. **23 May 1986**

ABOVE: DM 1178 was fitted with an electronic destination display by Wilts & Dorset which is clearly visible as it leaves Poole bus station. **23 May 1986**

RIGHT: Wilts & Dorset 1936 former DMS 2026 would eventually give the new owner eight years service which would be two years more than its time with LT. Seen standing in Poole bus station. **23 May 1986**

35

LEFT: DMS 325 was one of tw[o] similar vehicle in the Ensignbu[s] Sightseeing fleet to receive all ov[er] advertisements for The Trocade[ro] in 1986, it is parked at Trafalg[ar] Square between duties. **25 Ma[y] 1986**

BELOW LEFT: The secon[d] vehicle in Trocadero livery wa[s] DMS 353 seen here parked outsi[de] the establishment it is promotin[g]. **25 May 1986**

ABOVE: One of the few DMSs that did not pass to Ensignbu[s] was DMS 1834 which went to the dealer Allco Passenger Vehic[le] Sales of Ruislip. It was purchased by Evencost Ltd who set u[p] a rival London Sightseeing Tour company trading as 'Lond[on] Tour Company'. Their start point was Piccadilly where it [is] seen. **25 May 1986**

BELOW: Ensignbus DMS 315 received this all over advertisement for the Virgin Megastore for the 1986 season seen here at Piccadilly. After use in London it would be shipped with others for further use in Toronto Canada, unfortunately it broke loose during shipping and was badly damaged and thus written off after arrival. **25 May 1986**

BELOW: Another vehicle in the Evencost fleet was DM 1110 obtained fro[m] dealer Olympic Coachways, Stratton-on-the-Fosse. It too awaits custome[rs] at Piccadilly; the following month it would lose its roof and thus become a[n] open topper. Later in life it would operate sightseeing tours with Blue Triangl[e]. **25 May 1986**

36

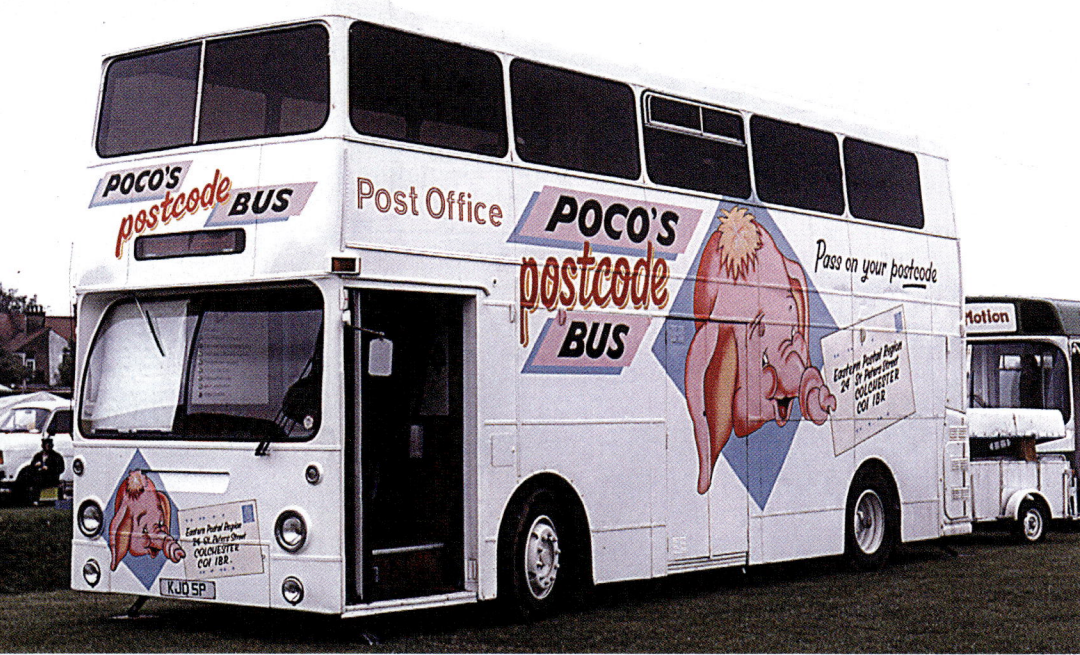

TOP: Ensignbus DMS 192 carrying Marks & Spencer livery at Piccadilly. This pass would later emigrate to Chicago for continued use on sightseeing tours. **25 May 1986**

ABOVE LEFT: DMS 1256 was illustrated in DMS ColourScene 1979 - 1984, following withdrawal by Hewitts Farm of Orpington it is seen here parked in the field next to the A21 as a billboard. **26 May 1986**

ABOVE: DMS 210 was owned for five years by Age Concern of Southwark often being seen in Camberwell garage. It is seen in use at the Peckham Rye gala. **31 May 1986**

LEFT: The Post Office Corporation (Eastern Region) would acquire three DMSs. The first acquired was DMS 2005 seen here at the Southend bus rally carrying its original livery as Poco's Postcode Bus. It was used to tour schools to encourage the use of Postcodes. Two of the three vehicles had a second staircase fitted at the rear. This bus still exists as a promotional unit for Epping Forest college. **1 June 1986**

DM 1797 being prepared for service by Nelson's of Wickford. Here is the final result complete with the NIBS fleetname outside their garage. **7 June 1986**

RIGHT: Premier of Cambridge operated DMSs on a Park and Ride service to the city. Here we find DMS 1983 speeding along outside Emmanuel College. **7 June 1986**

RIGHT: DMS 2192 takes on passengers at Peterborough bus station for the trip to Whittlesey the home village of its owner, Morleys. Acquired in early 1984 this would continue to work this route for 20 years and is still in occasional use in 2004. **7 June 1986**

RIGHT: Ambassador Coaches of Epping operated DMS 1655 for almost four years seen here in their yard at Thornwood Common in unusual livery with the then fashionable diagonal rear stripes. **14 June 1986**

ABOVE: SIACO Ltd based in Saffron Walden obtained DMS 434 as a mobile display unit. Following conversion it required testing as an HGV and had great difficulty passing the stringent brake test. It stands outside their factory specifically posed for the writer. **14 June 1986**

LEFT: Several DMSs in the Brandon fleet would be outstationed in Braintree bus park. DM 1023 still in LT red livery is behind DM 1217 which still carries the livery of its previous owner Florida Travel of Halstead. **14 June 1986**

BELOW LEFT: Brandon's would operate DMSs in their fleet for around fifteen years. Here DM 1003 stands in the corner of yard at Blackmore End in a simple yet attractive livery. **14 June 1986**

BELOW: The yard of Cuttings of Brockley Green was impossible to find without directions and involved traveling along narrow country lanes. Nevertheless the journey was well worthwhile to find this extremely smart DM 1067 shortly before its sale to Kettlewell of Retford. When first obtained by Cutting this bus had a tendency to lose its drive belts, but the problem was solved such that this bus is still active with Kettlewell in 2004. **14 June 1986**

41

ABOVE LEFT: In October 1985 General Foods of Banbury acquired DMS 294 as a promotional unit. Its first livery was to promote Bird's Desserts. Seen outside Tesco at Thurrock in this role. Eventually this bus would be sold to Ebdon of Sidcup for use as a hospitality unit. It was then sold to 'travellers' for cash and has disappeared without trace – any information on its current whereabouts would be very welcome by the author. **19 June 1986**

ABOVE: London Radiophone Ltd acquired DM 1673 for promotional purposes in 1985, although the company was based in London the bus was normally seen along the south coast. In this view is being used at Fontwell Park. **21 June 1986**

LEFT: DMS 439 was initially sold to Charles Coc Travel of Biggleswade in 1979, but in 1984 it passe to Ford's Travel of Gunnislake in Cornwall. Standing outside their depot the front shows pai damage from use along narrow lanes with hedge and low trees. **1 July 1986**

BELOW LEFT: Darleyford Coaches were based Upton Cross in Cornwall. They operated DMS 137 between 1979 and 1987. Note the retention of th centre exit doors and the LT style yellow entranc doors. **1 July 1986**

BELOW: DM 1726 was a much traveled vehicl In the previous volume it was pictured in Norwic Here it is again in Newton Abbot, Devon now owne by Roger Garrett Coaches, it would later pass t Filers of Ilfracombe before ending its days as hospitality unit with a Falmouth based trav agency. **1 July 1986**

42

LEFT: Positioned for the camera is DMS 2001 in the yard of Marsh's at Wincanton. This bus would later pass to Regency Tours in Bath for sightseeing work and its attractive number plate removed for separate sale. **3 July 1986**

BELOW LEFT: Sampson's Bus & Coach Travel of Cheshunt were successful in tendering for LRT routes in Hertfordshire, one such route being the 250 on which we find DMS 1881 at Waltham Abbey. **12 July 1986**

BELOW RIGHT: Another DMS in the Premier Travel fleet was DMS 2024 seen here at the cattle market terminus for the park and ride scheme. Each Premier Travel DMS carried advertising for different holiday destinations on each side. **12 July 1986**

RIGHT: Hedingham DMS 415 was shown in the first book in the original livery of predominately cream with red. Seen here in their Hedingham yard several years later it is now predominately red with cream and looking extremely smart. **12 July 1986**

43

ABOVE LEFT: Another vehicle in the Brandon fleet is DM 1097 seen in the Blackmore End yard. **12 July 1986**

ABOVE: As well as outstationing vehicles in Braintree bus park Brandon also kept vehicles at Cooks garage Braintree. Here we find the only MCW bodied DMS in their fleet DM 1707. **12 July 1986**

LEFT: Three contemporary double deckers in the yard of Motts, Stoke Mandeville, DMS 2226 stands between a former Reading Transport VR and a former WMPTE fleetline, of particular interest is that the WMPTE fleetline would have been displaced from its original fleet by DMS obtained from Ensignbus. **19 July 1986**

RIGHT: St Edwards Roman Catholic primary school in Sheerness acquired DMS 550 as school transport, seen here in the school grounds retaining its LT livery, but with the new owner's name in black lettering. It had been owned for 3½ years and would be repainted blue/yellow during the summer school holidays the following month. **20 July 1986**

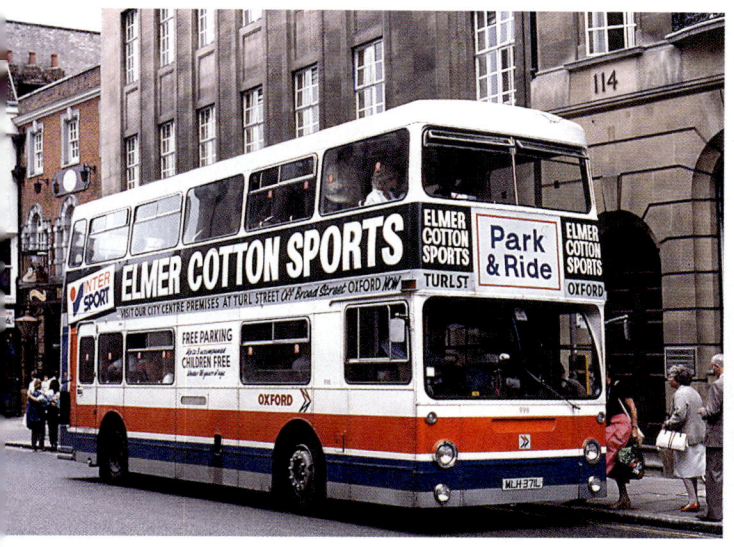

ABOVE LEFT: DMS 1371 was the newest DMS in the City of Oxford fleet seen collecting passengers on the Park and Ride service. This bus would last another year with Oxford before passing to Southend transport for further service. **26 July 1986**

ABOVE: Also picking up passengers in Oxford is DMS 1348. After sale by Oxford in 1988 this would be become a mobile advice centre in Cornwall. **26 July 1986**

LEFT: Ensignbus created a lot of comment when in 1986 they repainted a couple of DMSs into 7-Up livery, the paint effect of the bubbles was unique at the time and foreshadowed a step forward in paint schemes creating a particular visual impact. There was also a vending machine selling 7-Up drinks fitted over the centre exit steps. DMS 165 stands at the Trocadero. **26 July 1986**

RIGHT: Cream Line of Tonmawr, Gwent was a small welsh independent based in a small village east of Neath, not shown on many road maps, it being necessary to consult an OS Map to find its location for a visit. They obtained three DMSs to augment their fleet. DMS 1984 is parked in Neath bus station between duties. **2 August 1986**

45

ABOVE: The rural nature of the Cream Line depot is visible from this view of DM 982 positioned specially for the camera. This bus would later become a café and then a mobile home. It was last seen 'dumped' after a mechanical failure in a field near the France/Spain border, although it is rumored that it may still exist?. **2 August 1986**

ABOVE RIGHT: The third of the trio with Cream Line was DM 1022, note the simplified livery compared to DM 982. The final fate of this bus remains unknown. It was last reported as a promotional vehicle for the 'Instant Muscle' Fitness club in Manchester in 1992. **2 August 1986**

RIGHT: The 1986 visit to Swansea. Leaving the bus station is D Coaches DM 1052 was one of four vehicles acquired in 1985. It had previously operated for T&K Coaches of Ilford. **2 August 1986**

BELOW: Ensignbus C224, DM 1709 in Royal Wedding silver livery (Prince Andrew and Sarah Ferguson) seen on a very wet day in Wapping. **3 August 1986**

BELOW RIGHT: The Kent County Council acquired three DMSs for conversion into playbuses. DMS 1427 was allocated to Dover and used in this role for 3 years. The re-positioning of the front number plate in this way was unusual. **9 August 1986**

LEFT: Metrobus of Orpington was another small independent successful in securing an LRT contract for route 61 and route 361 was also added. The natural vehicle choice was the DMS. One week before the start of their contract the vehicles were in store in the Green Street Green garage. Here we find DMS 2056, DMS 2243 and DMS 1898 ready for their new life. **10 August 1986**

BELOW LEFT: Pleasurewood Hills is an American theme park at Corton just outside Lowestoft. They purchased DMS 326 to provide a courtesy bus service from the nearest railway station at Oulton Broad where it is seen collecting customers. **27 August 1986**

BELOW: The Waveney Playbus Association acquired DMS 358 in summer 1985. One year later it is all packed and about to depart from Lowestoft sea front. **28 August 1986**

LEFT: Mr Claireaux of Hadleigh ran a bus dealing business as well Partridge Coaches, he didn't often welcome enthusiasts into his yard. However on this occasion he allowed me access to see DMS 1647 in his own fleet and visible just behind in dealer stock is DMS 855 which was illustrated in DMS ColourScene 1979 -1984. **29 August 1986**

47

RIGHT: A short lived sightseeing operation around Richmond was run by Wealden Motor Services of Feltham using just two DMSs. This bus DMS 821 was sold to Wigley for scrap by Wealden, but passed immediately to Mr Claireaux for his dealer stock and was stored inside his shed for about 2 years to provide parts for his other DMSs. **29 August 1986**

BELOW: Looking like new is Osborne's of Tollesbury DM 1219. It had been number 3 in the Osborne's fleet since mid 1983 and would eventually be replaced by another DMS. It is seen outside its new home base. **29 August 1986**

BELOW RIGHT: Another DMS rumored to still exist, but unseen for several years is DMS 860. When first sold it went to the Bickers Action Enterprise Company and used for film work hence retention of the LT livery. The reason for the missing upper side window is because it had been used in a television advertisement for the then new Vauxhall Nova. In the advert the car appeared to drive through the bus, which was achieved by filming the car apparently entering the bus and then cutting to a stage mock-up. It awaits its next film role in the Coddenham yard. **29 August 1986**

BOTTOM: Another Kent County Council playbus was DMS 1613 which became the Thanet area bus. It was painted in 'Asterix the Gaul' livery and named the Viking Community Bus when photographed at its base outside Broadstairs. This bus would later pass to New York Apple Tours and like other former playbuses in New York be used as a static ticket sales office; in this case its new home would be on Broadway. **5 September 1986**

48

LEFT: The last of the three DMSs with Kent County Council was the Medway area playbus. DMS 661 was acquired for this role and was stored under cover in Chatham dockyard. It was moved outside for this photograph to be taken. **5 September 1986**

BELOW: A bus livery of black/grey may sound sombre, but DM 1138 with New Enterprise Coaches (Tonbridge) Ltd shows that this need not be the case. This bus was illustrated with Ebdons in the previous volume on London Sightseeing work with upper windows removed and blind box painted over. Two years later it is back in normal everyday service standing outside the Maidstone & District garage at Borough Green. When the company was taken over by M&D in 1988 this bus became a driver trainer with them for another 4 years. **5 September 1986**

BELOW LEFT: Penzance in the rain, DMS 72, DMS 679 and DMS 1526 owned by Western National carrying Cornish Busways as a fleetname represent their fleet of 38 DMSs many of which would go on to serve with other operators. These three formed part of the first batch which had originally been ordered by the Bristol Omnibus Company, but quickly diverted before use. **13 September 1986**

BELOW RIGHT: DMS 1502 was destined to be last DMS to leave the Western National fleet in Nov 1989 having been in the reserve store for twelve months, it also received the new blue/cream livery in 1988. Seen here arriving at Camborne garage. **13 September 1986**

49

RIGHT: Stevensons No. 31 seen here backing off the stand in Uttoxeter bus station was a heavily rebuilt DMS 1689 using parts from at least four other vehicles. Such was the amount of re-building that the bus qualified for a new registration number and it accordingly carries CBF31Y. **20 September 1986**

BELOW: Midland Red (North) Ltd based in Cannock received twenty DMSs from Western National. Most entered service in NBC green before being repainted. However, DMS 1516 was repainted, as shown here outside Cannock bus station. **20 September 1986**

RIGHT: DMS 1973 would achieve over eight years in service with Stevensons. It is about to leave their garage in Burton on Trent which was the former premises of the East Staffordshire District Council bus operation carrying an advertisement livery for Toons carpet warehouse. **20 September 1986**

50

ABOVE: One of the smartest DMSs owned by an independent operator was DMS 1548 with Castleways positioned here at the Winchcombe garage with an equally impressive background. This bus would have several further owners before returning to London to end its days as an open topper in the Big Bus sightseeing fleet. **11 October 1986**

CENTRE: After service with Youngs Coaches (see previous volume) DMS 2033 passed to the well known Cotswold operator Pulham & Sons of Bourton-on-the-Water. This was their only double decker and when acquired it was found to have a cracked engine block. Fortunately it was deemed worthwhile to repair and here it looks almost brand new, note also the chrome strip added to the front panel, a feature it retained with subsequent owners and still has in 2004. Seen at its Cotswold home. **11 October 1986**

RIGHT: Earlier in this book we saw DMS 550 in LT red livery with St. Edwards Roman Catholic Primary School in Sheerness. A few months later the repaint into blue and yellow 'starburst' livery was completed. Despite the repaint the bus would be replaced by a newer DMS in 1987 and DMS 550 would become a mobile technology unit. After this role it would become a mobile site office for a plant hire company and still performs this role in 2004. **25 October 1986**

South China – Guangzhou (Canton) 1993 – 1994

RIGHT: The headlights mounted on the centre panel identify this as an early DMS. Guangzhou No1 Bus Company 12-1388 is in fact DMS 142. This had previously been in the Argos fleet and was acquired by Citybus specifically for sending to Guangzhou it is about to leave the main bus station. **10 May 1993**

BELOW: DMS 142 now Guangzhou No1 Bus Company 12-1388 showing that both UK nearside doors have been paneled over, compare this with the photograph in DMS ColourScene Hong Kong. **10 May 1993**

BELOW LEFT: Guangzhou No1 Bus Company 5-1360 DMS 2178 squeezes between other vehicles and passengers in the main bus station advertising a brand of cigarettes. **10 May 1993**

BELOW : Also pictured in DMS ColourScene Hong Kong while with Citybus DMS 2178 is now in Guangzhou operating for the Guangzhou No1 Bus Company as 5-1360. **10 May 1993**

52

ABOVE LEFT: The non opening flat windscreens change the frontal appearance of DMS 2149; it stands in Guangzhou bus station while operating for the No.1 Bus Company as their 12-1364. **10 May 1993**

ABOVE: Fitted with new windscreens, but with opening vents is Guangzhou No.1 Bus Company 14-1358, DMS 2130 formerly D41 in the Citybus fleet, just visible behind is a former BVG Berlin MAN double decker. **26 April 1994**

LEFT: This is DM 1745 now Guangzhou No.1 Bus Company 14-1367 clearly a MCW bodied vehicle although it carries a registration plate which would later be transferred to DMS 796 causing some identity confusion. It stands in Guangzhou bus station between duties. **26 April 1994**

LEFT: DM 1745 now Guangzhou No.1 Bus Company 14-1367 showing the paneled over doors with a neat fitting window in the lower front side panel to allow the driver to see adjacent traffic. **26 April 1994**

ABOVE: Guangzhou No.1 Bus Company 14-1359 is DMS 2165 in all over advertisement livery for 'Skippy' stand in the busy Guangzhou bus station. **26 April 1994**

LEFT: This bus was previously an open topper in Hong Kong. Showing the rebuilt new square roof is DMS 220 now Guangzhou No.1 Bus Company 14-1382, it stands in the main road outside the bus station carrying an all ove advertisement for 'National'. **26 April 1994**

BELOW: Showing the re-positioned entrance door is DMS 2165 now in the ownership of the Guangzhou No.1 Bu Company and numbered 14-1359. **26 April 1994**

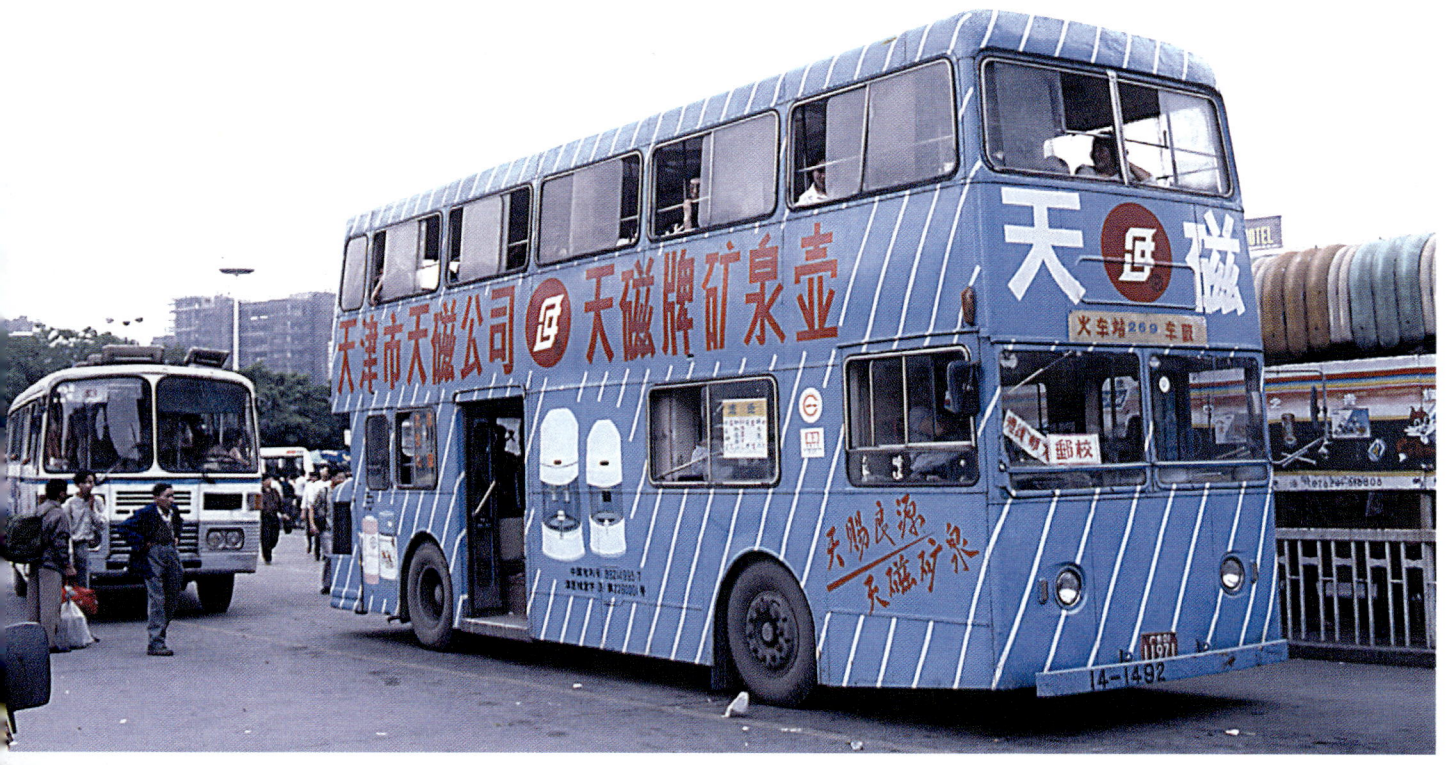

ABOVE: This is an unidentified DMS (can you help?) it is one of DMS 698, DMS 739 or DMS 785 and came from the KMB fleet via Speedybus hence the rebuilt lower front panel and new flat windscreen. It is now numbered 14-1492 in the fleet of the Guangzhou No 1 Bus Company and appeared to be in good condition. **26 April 1994**

LEFT: UK Nearside view in Guangzhou bus station of Guangzhou No.1 Bus Company 14-1492 showing the retention of the narrow front entrance door as converted by KMB. **26 April 1994**

LEFT: A busy scene at Guangzhou bus station as DM 1745 attempts to leave after a sudden rain shower. This bus is now 14-1367 in the fleet of the No.1 Bus Company. **26 April 1994**

55

United Kingdom – 1987

RIGHT: Earlier in this book DMS 1358 was pictured in WMPTE livery with Harris Bus Co. In mid 1986 it was painted by them into this all over advertisement livery for ASDA, it stands outside ASDA at Tilbury. **2 January 1987**

BELOW: Also pictured in DMS ColourScene 1979 - 1984 was DMS 392. Three years later it was one of two DMSs to pass from Chartercoach of Harwich to Jubilee Coaches of Stevenage. Seen here looking a little the worse for wear in Stevenage bus station, the lack of destination blind boxes does not help to inform potential customers. **31 January 1987**

LEFT: During the winter months Ensignbus would use surplus sightseeing buses on stage work if the need arose. Hence we find DMS 1444 in London Dungeon livery deputizing for a normal liveried bus such as that behind (DM 1101) at the well known terminus of route 62, Barking Gascoigne Road. **21 March 1987**

56

LEFT: Ensignbus had a contract with the Ford Motor Company, Dagenham for the provision of services using three vehicles, numbered EB 1, 2 & 3. Here EB 1 DMS 1844 stands outside the factory. **21 March 1987**

LEFT: SYPTE bought a batch of 29 fleetlines to a similar specification to DMSs. After sale ten passed to Grey Green who operated them on LRT route 173 under the fleetname EastenderBus OKW526R stands at the route terminus at Becontree Heath Bus Station. **21 March 1987**

BELOW LEFT: Numerically the last of the SYPTE 'DMS style' fleetlines and the only one to receive an 'S' registration plate was SHE507S seen here in Lower Regent Street while operating London sightseeing tours with Cityrama. This bus would subsequently be converted to partial open top and be used to inaugurate a sightseeing tour in Coventry. **29 March 1987**

BELOW: Tamworth and two Midland Red North DMSs illustrate the old WNOC green livery on DMS 1528 and the new red livery on DMS 1516. I didn't know at the time of my visit that all the Midland Red North DMSs would be abruptly withdrawn from service the following day!. **25 April 1987**

57

ABOVE LEFT: Burton-on-Trent sees Stevensons DMS 2034 in an all over advertisement livery for Peter Smith Sports Cars Ltd. This bus would later see further service with Midland Red East in Leicester. **25 April 1987**

ABOVE: The penultimate day of DMS operation by Midland Red North finds recently repainted DMS 1526 standing in Tamworth. The repaint demonstrates that the decision taken to withdraw this bus and the other DMSs the following day was taken at very short notice. **25 April 1987**

LEFT: DMS 1512 with Midland Red North seen here in Tamworth never received red livery. It would pass to Midland Red East, but only in the role of a driver training bus. **25 April 1987**

LEFT: London Sightseeing Tours painted DMS 1944 in this very attractive livery to promote the new developments in London Dockland. It waits at the Victoria pick up point alongside Victoria station. **10 May 1987**

58

LEFT: Earlier in this book DM 1830 was pictured with Waterhouse Coaches. Two years later it had joined the fleet of New Enterprise and stands in their Tonbridge yard. **16 May 1987**

BELOW: Still looking like it was owned by LT, but DMS 806 was in fact owned by the Transport & General Workers Union. It has been driven out of its home, Wandsworth garage to allow this photograph to be taken. **22 May 1987**

BOTTOM LEFT: DM 995 backs into Icknield School to collect school children for the afternoon journey home. It is a sad fact that it would be inappropriate to stand outside a school taking photographs in 2004. The bus was bought by House's Watlington Buses in August 1984. In August 1987 the bus would pass to Globe Heath in Cardiff and later in a strange move revert to full LT red livery with Venture Travel of Cardiff. **22 May 1987**

BOTTOM RIGHT: Cedar Coaches of Bedford always produce an interesting fleet of second hand double deckers and they have equally interesting new minibuses and coaches. DM 1827 was very kindly moved outside for me by the owner for facilitate this photograph. Note the window in place of the centre exit door is slightly different from the others. **23 May 1987**

ABOVE LEFT: Five DMSs operate[d] with the Rolls Royce Eagle engin[e]. Of these three were sold for furth[er] service to three different independen[ts] via the dealer Smith's coaches [of] Shenington. Accordingly a netwo[rk] was established between them [to] exchange information on the[ir] upkeep. One of these was DMS 21[2] which passed to SM Ementon [of] Cranfield seen here in its origin[al] livery in their yard next to DM 9[79] still in LT red. **23 May 1987**

ABOVE: Earlier in this bo[ok] Ensignbus executive hospitality b[us] DMS 852 was featured in its origin[al] orangey red livery. One year lat[er] and a return visit to Purfleet finds it [in] this attractive maroon. **25 May 19**[87]

LEFT: Still in LRT ownership D[MS] 1102 was used on a shuttle b[us] service from Greenwich to th[e] Thames Barrier. Originally white th[e] bus received this red livery and th[e] name MV Royal Daffodil in sprin[g] 1985. It waits to depart at the Barrie[r]. **25 May 1987**

LEFT: A corner of the yard belongin[g] to Premier of Cambridge finds DM[S] 1989 and DMS 1983 in company wi[th] a Bristol Lodekka. **30 May 1987**

60

ABOVE: The station yard at Warnham is the setting for this view of DMS 1667 in the fleet of Horsham coaches. One always had to approach the station from the west on Sundays because the level crossing next to the yard remained shut on this day. **6 June 1987**

ABOVE RIGHT: Horsham coaches were not alone in taking delivery of a DMS that had operated previously for WMPTE. Here DMS 1308 is positioned in Warnham station yard only one month after acquisition. **6 June 1987**

RIGHT: I am grateful to Trent Motor Traction Co Ltd who by prior arrangement had agreed to drive out their two DMSs especially for me during this Sunday visit. The two vehicles had been purchased from The South Wales Transport Co Ltd the previous year and spent several months being extensively refurbished. DMS 2019 stands in front of DMS 1991 outside their Derby Meadow Road garage both looking resplendent. **7 June 1987**

BELOW: The full effects of the extensive refurbishment are evident in this view of DMS 1991 outside the Meadow Road garage of the Trent Motor Traction Co. Ltd. **7 June 1987**

61

LEFT: Derby City Transport sold the three Dennis Dominators to Thamesdown Transport and received three DMSs in exchange. This is DM 2195 freshly painted on view in the garage during an open day demonstrating how they would be attached to a recovery truck following a breakdown. **7 June 1987**

LEFT: St Ignatius College in Enfield bought DM 1117 for school transport and it retained LT red livery for its life with the college. It is seen in the college grounds. This bus would later pass to Big Bus for sightseeing work in London. **21 June 1987**

BELOW LEFT: Sampson's Bus and Coach Travel painted DM 930 into this eye catching livery to advertise the Cheshunt and Waltham Telegraph and Enfield Gazette. Seen here on LF service 217B at Waltham Cross. **June 1987**

BELOW RIGHT: Following the success of DMS 2163 illustrated in the first book, Mayne's of Manchester acquired two further DMSs from Stevensons in 1985. DMS 2131 was one of these seen in an attractive version of their livery opposite the garage. **27 June 1987**

62

RIGHT: The second vehicle acquired by Payne's from Stevensons in 1985 was DMS 135 seen here taking on passengers at Manchester, Piccadilly in yet another livery variation. **27 June 1987**

BELOW: Five DMSs from the Youngs fleet joined others with Yelloway Motor Services at Rochdale. Unfortunately this once respected coach company was in terminal decline and when buses failed they were often set aside and stripped for spares to keep others going. Here DMS 2025 has succumbed to that fate in their garage. A far cry from its smart condition with Youngs illustrated in the previous book. **27 June 1987**

BELOW RIGHT: By this date photographing Yelloway DMSs in service was hard with frequent gaps in the services. A wait of over two hours at this stop in Albert Square Manchester was necessary before the arrival of DMS 2028 another vehicle previously with Youngs. **27 June 1987**

RIGHT: DMS 1616 was kept at the LCBS Dorking garage on whose forecourt it stands. The bus was owned by Cairnmark Ltd as a publicity/hospitality unit. The bus would later pass to Olympus Cameras before being exported to France. **4 July 1987**

63

LEFT: Pardes House school in Finchley ran four buses on school runs. The fleet is seen at the school wi[th] DMS 664 heading the line. **9 July 1987**

ABOVE: Following the success of their two DMSs purchased in 1984 Shorey Travel purchased DM 999 [in] 1986 and others would follow. All Shorey vehicles carried all over advertisements and DM 999 displays th[at] for the local British Leyland dealer. The orange engine cover is sometimes deemed to be the Shorey fle[et] livery. Just visible behind in their yard is DMS 1893. **9 July 1987**

BELOW LEFT: DMS 1981 was bought by North Thames Gas to become a mobile showroom for gas fire[s]. It was also registered with the appropriate cherished plate '1 NTG'. It is seen here outside the Great Mi[lls] superstore in Ashford Middlesex. The fires on board could be actually switched on and in consequence t[he] bus had a 9" chimney on the roof which required lowering before the vehicle was moved otherwise it wou[ld] not fit under many London bridges. **9 July 1987**

ABOVE: Another former WMPTE DMS to see furth[er] service was DMS 1290 which joined the Bath Cent[re] for Voluntary Service and named 'The Bath Bus'. Th[is] would be later repainted pale blue and parked for ma[ny] years in the corner of Bath coach park. Here it is se[en] in original condition at its first home, Pickfords yard [in] Bath. **12 July 1987**

LEFT: The dealer Olympic Coachways acquired DM[S] 2030 which then passed to Filer's Travel of Ilfracomb[e]. It is seen here at Church Street Ilfracombe. The fin[al] fate of this bus is unknown, it is thought to have bee[n] exported to New York Apple Tours, but there ha[ve] been no reported sightings of its arrival. **14 July 19**[87]

64

TOP LEFT: Another DMS which passed through Olympic Coachways was DMS 1911 seen here in the Bristol yard of Glenvic. Note the neatly painted out destination boxes. This bus still exists in 2004 with a community group in Abingdon. **20 July 1987**

TOP RIGHT: A third DMS from Olympic Coachways was DMS 1942 which passed to Axe Vale Coaches of Biddisham. It stands in their yard with advertising for the Farmers Tavern night spot at Brean Leisure Park. **20 July 1987**

ABOVE: Maybury's Coaches of Cranborne ran London Sightseeing Tours as well as local routes. This view of their Cranborne base shows DMS 1962 in local fleet livery undergoing maintenance. In the corner are the remains of DMS 1543 one of several acquired solely for spares. **21 July 1987**

LEFT: The only DMS to operate on the Isle of Wight is DM 1108 with the County Council. This bus was one of many converted by BSTE Ltd into mobile technology units to tour schools. It is seen on a wet day on the Quay at Newport. After disposal by the council this bus would serve as a static grandstand before being finally broken up and scrapped in 2003. **22 July 1987**

65

LEFT: One of the very early sales of DMS in 1980 was DMS 1402 which found its way via Ensignbus to Charlton Services where it was a regular performer on the run into Oxford on market days and Saturdays. This view was taken in its home village. **23 July 1987**

CENTRE LEFT: House's Watlington Buses sold up in August 1987. One month earlier their two fleetlines DM 995 and DM 109 pose in the doorway of their garage. Note the City of Oxford sign was still above the door long after the company had departed from this site. **23 July 1987**

BOTTOM LEFT: DMS 702 had been operating for Davie's of Rye for almost seven years when it was captured on film in Station Road, New Romney. **15 August 1987**

BELOW: Events European Ltd were an early user of the DMS in a hospitality role having acquired DMS 299 in autumn 198_. It was kept at Waddon Station. Note the panelled-over lower deck windows. It is waiting at traffic lights at the junction of Commerce Way and Purley Way, Croydon having just been refueled at the local petrol/diesel garage the nearest with a high enough roof to accommodate the bus. **23 August 1987**

LEFT: The D Coaches garage at Tycroes with DMS 1880 pausing whilst en route between Swansea and Llandeilo. **29 August 1987**

BELOW LEFT: In spring 1987 Ensignbus carried out a conversion to DMS 1943 on behalf of Philips Consumer Electronics. This involved fitting a new 'Enterprise' front and removing the rear two thirds of the roof to create a stage upstairs. The lower deck windows were paneled over and Philips products were displayed downstairs. It then toured seaside resorts during the summer. This location is Great Yarmouth Pleasure Beach. Although it has been stored in the open for many years, this bus still exists. **8 September 1987**

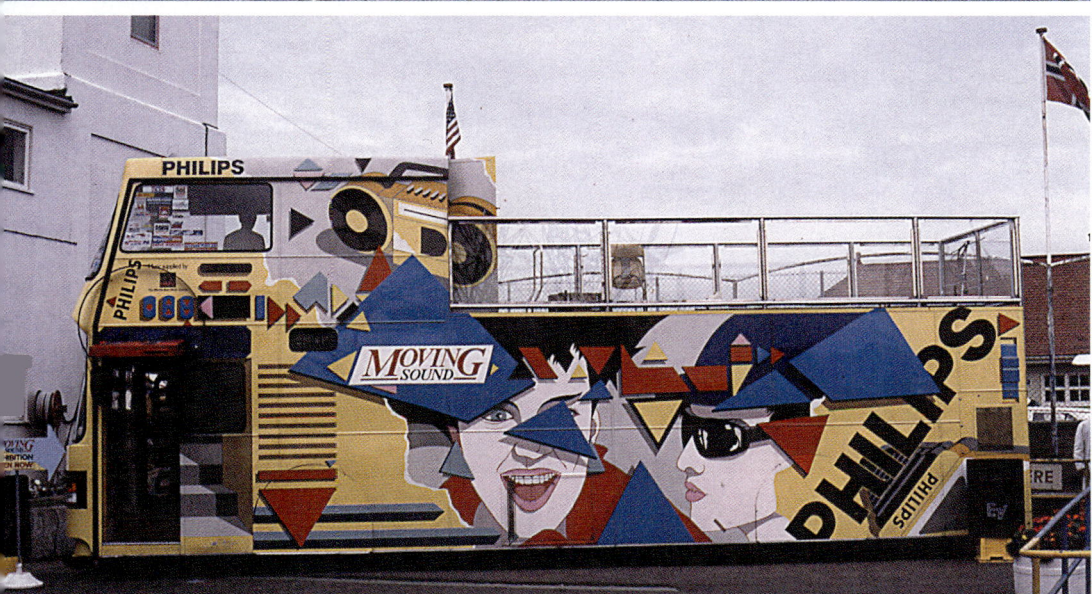

BOTTOM LEFT: This is DM 1081 freshly painted in the yard of Swaffham Coachways. The bus had operated in LT red for the previous four years (see DMS ColourScene 1979-1984). Having operated for so long in red it was ironic that the bus was sold only six months after this view was taken. **10 September 1987**

BOTTOM RIGHT: Harlow Council for Voluntary Service operated DMS 276 as a playbus for nearly twenty years. At various times after repaint it was used in plain blue until money could be found to replace the rainbow stripes. It is seen here in full livery outside Harlow Town Hall. **27 September 1987**

67

LEFT: A couple of visits were necessary before I managed to photograph DMS 185 with Westrings at their West Wittering farm base. This bus would later return to London and operate with Big Bus. **4 October 198**

BELOW LEFT: When LRT announced the tender results for a new operation based Bexley it was a surprise to learn that a new low cost subsidiary of London Buses would be set up with its own identity and livery Bexleybus was the chosen name and addition to new Leyland Olympians diverted from a Greater Manchester order the other double deckers would be DMSs. Some were returned from Clydeside in exchange for Routemasters and others were refurbished examples still owned Ensignbus gained the refurbishment contract and here we see DMS 2125 and DM 1146 nearing completion in the Purfleet yard. **25 October 1987**

68

OPPOSITE PAGE:

CENTRE RIGHT: DM 1710 was illustrated in the previous volume in use with Ebdons. Three years later it stands in the Purfleet yard of Ensignbus awaiting shipment to Chicago. Note the fitting of the offside door to facilitate use in the USA. **25 October 1987**

BOTTOM: It was inevitable that many DMSs would pass through Ensignbus several times. Standing in their Purfleet yard after return from their original purchasers is World Education bus DMS 136 and former A1 DMS 2038. The latter was evidently just returned from a period of hire to Solent Blue Line as shown by their fleetname on the front of the existing A1 livery. Both vehicles would be resold for further use. **25 October 1987**

THIS PAGE:

TOP RIGHT: A visit to Ensignbus at Purfleet would always produce a few surprises. Here is DMS 1469 being converted for The Commercial Presentations Group who would in turn lease it to the Department of Employment. A new 'Enterprise' front is being fitted together with extensive bodywork modifications. A picture of the completed vehicle appears later in this book. **25 October 1987**

RIGHT: Surrounded by Zippy minibuses in Preston bus station is Mercer's of Grimsargh DMS 2222. This was the sole DMS in their fleet although they also operated two similar ex SYPTE fleetlines from the OKW...R batch. **November 1987**

BELOW: The ATL group set up a new subsidiary to operate routes won by tender around Pudsey Leeds. The fleetname was Airebus although the legal name was Sheffield United Transport and the operation ran for less than twelve months. DMSs were used from a variety of sources although many came via Yelloway Motor services another company in the ATL group. DMS 2031 is seen outside Pudsey Town hall. **21 November 1987**

BELOW RIGHT: Also ex Yelloway DMS 2027 is now No. 42 in the Airebus fleet it was caught by the camera in appaling light at Lidget Hill Pudsey. **21 November 1987**

69

LEFT: Several Airebus DMS came from Carlton dealers t whom they had been sold b Midland Red North, one such wa DMS 1650 was entered servic with its new owner earlier i November. Pudsey town centr is the location of this view **21 November 1987**

CENTRE LEFT: Few Airebus DMS carried fleetnames at the time of m visit. One that did was DMS 1611. stands at the entrance to the Airebu yard rented from Hargreaves Pudsey. **21 November 1987**

LEFT: Two of the DMS withdrawn abruptly by Midlar Red North passed to Uni Coaches of Clayworth. The unusual livery is demonstrated DMS 1659 in Retford bus stati while operating a local tow service. **28 November 1987**

ABOVE: The other DMS in the Unity fleet was DMS 1645 seen here at their Clayworth yard. **28 November 1987**

RIGHT: Lincoln City Transport bought four DMSs from Warrington in July 1987. A brief stop in Lincoln after my visit to Retford found DMS 1490 in the bus station which being under cover is somewhat dark. **28 November 1987**

RIGHT: Another conversion by BSTE Ltd was DMS 2238 which by 1987 was kept at the Polytechnic of the South Bank as the Open College Technobus. In this winter view it is making a visit to Woolwich College in Charlton. **December 1987**

71

USA – New York 1994

RIGHT: Known locally as 'Super 16' this is New York Apple Tours No.16, previously with Metrobus of Orpington and originally DMS 1977. This vehicle was rarely unfit and accordingly kept the same fleetnumber throughout its time in New York. It is loading up in Times Square. **30 September 1994**

CENTRE LEFT: New York Apple Tours No.10 was DMS 1839 which was still carrying its UK number plate when seen in Times Square. **30 September 1994**

BELOW RIGHT: Also carrying its UK registration plate is New York Apple Tours No.1 a former SYPTE look alike fleetline originally OKW510R parked between tours in Times Square. **30 September 1994**

BOTTOM: DM953 in all over advertisement livery for Kodak when captured on film in Times Square as New York Apple Tours No.3. This bus was identified by the unique treatment of the rearmost upper side with small infill panel. **30 September 1994**

72

RIGHT: Inside the original New York Apple Tours depot at 59th Street underneath Broadway. From left to right are DM 1720 with canvas roof, DMS 1984 with clear Perspex roof panels and similarly equipped DM 1015. Only DM 1015 had seen service by this date. **1 October 1994**

BELOW: A former London Sightseeing Tours DM which had three chrome rails at the rear mounted above an upper side panel. This is DM 1004 now New York Apple Tours No.4 standing in their 59th Street depot. **1 October 1994**

BELOW RIGHT: New York Pier 17 has been converted into a shopping and eating area similar to London's Covent Garden. Here New York Apple Tours No.30 DMS 1982 stops during a rain shower. **1 October 1994**

LEFT: It is still raining as DMS 1873 New York Apple Tours No.15 picks up passengers in Times Square. **1 October 1994**

73

LEFT: The Battery Park stop at the southern end of Manhattan was the stop for ferries to the Statue of Liberty and buses paused here for the lunch stop for crews. New York Apple Tour No.20, DM 1118 waits to leave for the second part of the Downtown Tour. **3 October 1994**

BELOW LEFT: This DM 2101 being prepared for service in the depot of New York Apple Tours. **4 October 1994**

BELOW: A line up of vehicles in the 59 Street depot of New York Apple Tours from left to right are DMS 1984, DM 1015, DM 2182, DMS 2407, DMS 2119, DMS 1836 and DMS 1447. **4 October 1994**

BOTTOM: New York Times Square sees Apple Tours No.25 DMS 2188 in use with full roof albeit with centre Perspex panels. Note the removal of the upper centre window. **4 October 1994**

74

RIGHT: With lettering for the Uptown and Harlem tour DMS 372 stands in Times Square carrying the initial Apple Tours livery including a blue band. **4 October 1994**

BELOW: New York Battery Park and DM 1004 parked for a lunch stop is passed by DM 118. The building behind is the Museum of the American Indian, the entrance to which had been used in the film GhostBusters. **4 October 1994**

BOTTOM LEFT: DMS 1873 is now New York Apple Tours No.15 alongside Battery Park at the southern tip of Manhattan. **4 October 1994**

BOTTOM RIGHT: New York Apple Tours No.7 DM 935 with a full load as it leaves Battery Park in New York. The treatment of the rear upper deck is typical of former Cityrama vehicles, ie. a solid panel. **4 October 1994**

75

United Kingdom – 1988

RIGHT: DMS 1652 was first sold to Hale Trent Cakes of Clevendon for staff transport. In 1983 it passed to British Aerospace at Filton to undertake a similar role. Access to their site was very difficult, nevertheless that is the location of this view. **15 January 1988**

RIGHT: The first day of the new Bexleybus operation finds DM 1146 carrying new fleet number 101 at Bexleyheath Clock Tower on route 229. **16 January 1988**

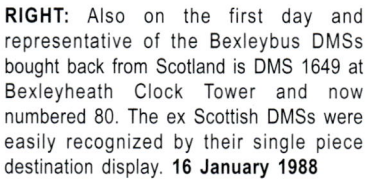

RIGHT: Also on the first day and representative of the Bexleybus DMSs bought back from Scotland is DMS 1649 at Bexleyheath Clock Tower and now numbered 80. The ex Scottish DMSs were easily recognized by their single piece destination display. **16 January 1988**

76

ABOVE LEFT: Earlier in this book DMS 392 was pictured looking a little sad. A year later and it has been repainted by Jubilee Coaches into this all over advertisement for the Allied Superstore, seen parked outside their depot. **24 January 1988**

ABOVE: Both DMSs in this view of the New Enterprise yard at Tonbridge had operated for Keenan's of Coalhall near Ayr, but returned to Ensignbus in November 1987. They were quickly re-sold, hence the adverts for the Ayr Advertiser on DMS 1614 and the blue/white Keenan livery on DMS 648. **30 January 1988**

LEFT: The newest DMS in the Metrobus of Orpington fleet, DMS 2243 carried this all over advertisement livery for Saunders Abbot for four years. It waits in Eltham station between journeys on LRT route 61 to Bromley. **13 March 1988**

LEFT: St Edwards Roman Catholic Primary School at Sheerness again. DMS 550 pictured earlier was replaced by DMS 2164 which was one of two DMSs returned to Ensignbus by Turner's of Brown Edge Staffordshire. Unlike DMS 550 the bus carries a much more restrained version of their blue/yellow livery. **13 March 1988**

77

LEFT: Earlier in this book DMS 192 was pictured in plain NBC red Swansea. When South Wales so their DMSs Wilts & Dorset obtaine four of them. One was DMS 192 looking extremely smart in the ne W&D livery when operating Bournemouth. **9 April 1988**

CENTRE LEFT: The origin livery carried by Barrow Boroug Transport Ltd DMSs was depicte earlier in this book. Three yea later the livery has been th subject of updating. DMS 2174 ar DMS 2175 seen at the garage **14 April 1988**

BELOW: A member of the BB staff very kindly took me to We Shore Road in DMS 2041 to g this photograph of the new liver **14 April 1988**

RIGHT: All ten DMSs remaining with Hants and Dorset passed to Cumberland Motor Services in October 1987. DMS 2203 seen here in Carlisle still carries the later H&D livery. **14 April 1988**

78

RIGHT: Dumfries by the river and Western Scottish R824, DMS 1917 is parked between duties in the plain white/grey/black livery. **15 April 1988**

BELOW: Well known Scottish independent James Liddell of Auchinleck bought three DMSs. The two seen here, DMS 1847 and DMS 1894 were fairly standard. The third numbered D1 was DM 1199 with a Rolls Royce engine that was frequently unserviceable as it was during this visit. **15 April 1988.**

BELOW RIGHT: Western Scottish Omnibuses had owned DM 1703 for five years when this photograph was taken as it leaves Cumnock bus station for the journey to Ayr. The new livery suits the vehicle well. **16 April 1988**

LEFT: The yard at Kilmarnock garage would see large numbers of DMSs. Here on a very wet day we see DMS 1695 in original red/cream colours alongside DMS 1986 in white/grey/black, note the different treatment to the destination displays. **16 April 1988**

79

ABOVE LEFT: DMS 1915 shows the 'normal' triangular Scottish destination display alongside DMS 1509 whilst standing in Kilmarnock garage yard. The final fate of DMS 1915 is unknown after it left the Cudworth re-sale yard of PVS in 1998. **16 April 1988**

ABOVE: A1 Service operated several DMSs. Here DMS 2161 owned by James Brown & Son, Dreghorn stands outside their garage. **19 April 1988**

LEFT: The plant yard of Melville, Dundas & Whitson at Paisley is the location of this view of DM 1713 which was used as a mobile site office particularly in areas subject to vandalism. **19 April 1988**

LEFT: Graham's Bus Services of Paisley would operate twenty different DMSs and were constantly updating the fleet by obtaining newer examples as they became available. Here D1, DMS 2137, stands out of use and would be sold shortly going on to have several more owners. **19 April 1988**

80

LEFT: One of the first trips made by converted DMS 1469 (see picture earlier in this book) was to Scotland. I came across it purely by chance parked in George Square, Glasgow. **19 April 1988**

CENTRE LEFT: Being used to tour the UK by the Department of Employment is DMS 1469 seen in Glasgow, George Square, it is hard to believe that this is a DMS such is the radical conversion. **19 April 1988**

LEFT: Marshall's of Ballieston bought two DMSs from Graham's and operated them in Graham's livery with their own fleetname added. Here the pair DMS 2057 and DMS 1451 are positioned for this photograph. **19 April 1988**

81

LEFT: Another vehicle previously owned b[y] Graham's was DMS 668 seen here in the ya[rd] of its new operator Wilson's of Carnwath, unlik[e] the vehicle illustrated next the centre exit doo[rs] have been removed. **19 April 1988**

LEFT: DMS 558 was illustrated in DM[S] ColourScene 1979 -1984 as a training bus w[ith] Brighton Corporation. Four years later it ha[d] returned to passenger service and reache[d] Wilson's of Carnwath. Note the modified a[ir] intake grills on the front panel a modificatio[n] carried out by Brighton. **19 April 1988**

BELOW LEFT: Shortly after a heavy show[er] three A1 Service vehicles stand to the rear [of] Kilmarnock bus station. Nearest the came[ra] is DMS 2046 owned by A Hunter of Dreghor[n]. **20 April 1988**

BELOW: J C Stewart of Stevenston was t[he] owner of DMS 2037 seen here specially pos[ed] outside his garage. **20 April 1988**

82

ABOVE: Clyde Coast Services of Saltcoats purchased DMS 665 from Graham's and painted it in this livery which is similar to that of A1. The fitting of a large front bumper is unusual. **20 April 1988**

ABOVE RIGHT: Positioned specially for me and fresh out of the paintshop and still awaiting application of fleetnames on the sides is DMS 2214 owned by J McKinnon in their Kilmarnock yard. **20 April 1988**

RIGHT: A return visit to the plant yard of Melville, Dundas & Whitson at Paisley to find that the company had kindly managed to move DM 713 for this photograph. **21 April 1988**

RIGHT: Highland Omnibuses bought two consecutively numbered DMSs in 1983. They operated for a time in Thurso, but by 1988 both had been re-allocated to Inverness where DMS 1440 now K350 is seen in Tomnahurich Street. **21 April 1988**

83

ABOVE: The second DMS in the Highland Omnibuses fleet was DMS 1441 now K351, seen here at the garage in Inverness. **22 April 1988**

ABOVE RIGHT: Earlier in this book we saw DMS 1528 with Midland Red North still in WNOC green livery. A year later and it is seen in the yard of Redwatch Travel, East Calder. **22 April 1988**

RIGHT: Ensignbus executive hospitality unit DMS 852 has been repainted again in connection with its use to support the Kaliber racing team. It stands in the Purfleet yard. **7 May 1988**

RIGHT: For many years DMS 1923 would operate in a white based livery for the Hollywood Nightclub. However here it is seen in the Ensignbus Purfleet yard in the original black based livery. **7 May 1988**

84

LEFT: For the 1988 summer season Philips bought a second DMS to tour with DMS 1943 (pictured earlier). The vehicle selected was DM 1800 seen here with DMS 1943 on one of its first outings at the Hempstead Valley Shopping Centre in Kent. **14 May 1988**

BELOW: This view taken at Woburn Leisure Park shows how DM 1800 and DMS 1943 were positioned together when in use. Note also that a trailer towed by one bus is positioned between the buses to create an even larger upper stage. Note also that DMS 1943 now has a sliding roof fitted. **21 May 1988**

BOTTOM LEFT: Surrey County Council also had a DMS converted into a mobile technology bus by BSTE Carlton. DMS 1842 is seen at the Highway House depot West Ewell yard showing that it received sponsorship support from British Aerospace. **27 May 1988**

BOTTOM RIGHT: London Buslines DM 962 waits to turn into Alperton station while operating on LRT route 79. **28 May 1988**

85

LEFT: Following the successf[ul] operation of DMS 2005, The Po[st] Office Corporation (Eastern Region) acquired a second DMS. DMS 198[8] was painted as the 'Write it' bus [to] encourage school children to writ[e] letters. It is on display at the Southe[rn] bus rally. **5 June 1988**

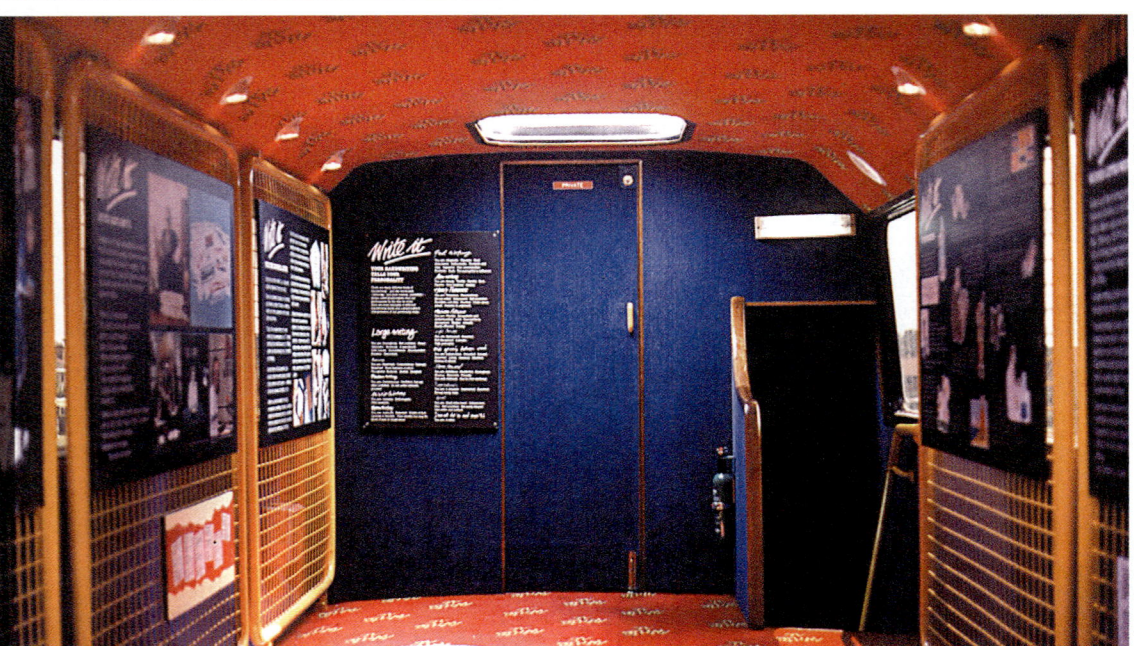

CENTRE: Upper deck of DMS 198[8] looking forward showing th[e] extensive use of carpeting wi[th] appropriate lettering and the new ro[of] light. Two Post Office vehicle[s] including this one, had a secon[d] staircase fitted at the rear to facilita[te] circulation of visitors. **5 June 198[8]**

BELOW: DMS 2005 with the Po[st] Office Corporation showing th[e] trailer attached and the revise[d] livery, it is in use at Stevenag[e] day. **12 June 1988**

ABOVE LEFT: This is DMS 461 owned by the London Borough of Richmond Education Department and used to tour schools. Like DMS 1842 it also received sponsorship support from British Aerospace. Seen at Hampton Junior School. **24 June 1988**

ABOVE RIGHT: Hornsby Travel Service would operate DMSs for over twenty years. DM 1181 was the first DMS to be acquired in 1981 and remained in the fleet until 2003. It is seen in their Ashby yard. **25 June 1988**

CENTRE LEFT: DM 1086 was also acquired by Hornsby Travel Service in 1981, but was to be sold relatively early in 1988. However it would operate with subsequent owners for many more years. Note the retention of the centre exit doors in this view at the Ashby base. **25 June 1988**

LEFT: DM 1137 had been owned by Hornsby Travel Service for over three years when it was caught operating on a local service in Ashby High Street. **25 June 1988**

87

RIGHT: DMS 2082 has received new Grimsby Cleethorpes Transport livery unlike the vehicle behind when seen in Grimsby. **25 June 1988**

BELOW: DMS 768 now Grimsby No. 17 pictured in Grimsby wearing the new GCT livery. **25 June 1988**

ABOVE: DMS 2095 seen Grimsby still wearing original livery **25 June 1988**

LEFT: London Buses Group Systems also had a DMS converted by BSTE Carlton for the OPE Project and could provide emergency computer facilities any computer systems failed. The vehicle in question was DM 115 and it was displayed here at typically wet Showbus rally shortly after the conversion was complete **3 July 1988**

LEFT: Another By Election saw DMS 2023 sporting a new livery to reflect 'New Labour' with the red rose now being prominent. It is seen outside Labour's Kensington office. **9 July 1988**

ABOVE LEFT: Ensignbus DMS 353 was repainted in 1988 to publicise the Rock Tour of London which operated twice daily. It stands at the start point in Regent Street. **9 July 1988**

ABOVE: Rear view of Ensignbus DMS 353 in Regent Street showing a Rock musician. **9 July 1988**

LEFT: DMS 464 was first used by Infradex Ltd, Hoddesdon as staff transport. In 1982 it passed to Mr J Taylor (Puckeridge Caravans) and used as a non mobile storeshed. Seen here at Puckeridge in very cramped conditions and very faded condition. **16 July 1988**

LEFT: DMS 2094 passed from Wiffens's coaches to R W Dew & Son in mid 1987. It is seen at the Somersham base devoid of fleetnames. **16 July 1988**

LEFT 3255: Note the different livery scheme on R W Dew & Son's second DMS. DMS 2152 carrying Dews Dekka fleetname is parked at the Wood Green animal shelter. **16 July 1988**

BELOW LEFT: DMS 2232 was originally sold to Thamesdown Transport but was returned to Ensignbus after being damaged. It was repaired and subsequently sold to Morley's of Whittlesey to join DMS 2192. Seen in Whittlesey in original livery. **16 July 1988**

BELOW: Youngs Coaches of Rampton bought DMS 1681 for spares in February 1985, over three years later its remains were still to be found in their yard as illustrated here. **16 July 1988**

90

LEFT: Chesterfield 160, DMS 553 numerically the first in their DMS fleet of sixteen. It is standing in Vicar Lane Chesterfield en route to Clay Cross with appropriate advertising. Behind is a Chesterfield fleetline in the new yellow and blue livery. **23 July 1988**

CENTRE LEFT: Also the first numerically, but this time in the Derby City Transport fleet is No.253 DMS 440 taking on passengers in Cornmarket. At this time it had been owned by Derby for over eight years and would in fact be withdrawn in October 1988. **23 July 1988**

CENTRE RIGHT: Derby 258, DMS 466 in Derby Market Place. This was one of the initial trial batch fitted from new with two piece glider front doors. **13 August 1988**

BOTTOM LEFT: DMS 2182 became Derby 247 when it was one of three DMSs bought from Thamesdown Transport in exchange for three Dominators. It is taking on passengers at Derby market Place. **13 August 1988**

BOTTOM RIGHT: Leicester City centre sees Astill & Jordan DMS 2043 waiting to depart on service 94 to Ratby. This month the Company would be taken over by Midland Fox. **13 August 1988**

91

ABOVE: DMS 1552 had been a very early sale and first operated for CK Coaches in Cardiff. After sale it passed via Stevensons to Astill & Jordan Ltd and received this unusual livery for the joint operation of Hylton & Dawson routes complete with HA fleet name on the side. Seen in Leicester. **13 August 1988**

ABOVE RIGHT: A third Astill & Jordan DMS in Leicester and the third different livery. DMS 2051 carries an all over advertisement livery for the Thomas's amusement centre. **13 August 1988**

RIGHT: Earlier in this book DMS 294 was illustrated in its original silver livery, a couple of years later it has gained this revised livery with General Foods. It stands outside Regents College in Regents Park London. The company said the registration 'JGF' was very appropriate because it was driven by John of General Foods. **21 August 1988**

BOTTOM LEFT: Taylor's of Sutton Scotney had previously purchased vehicles from Graham's Paisley and had been very pleased with them. Accordingly they bought three DMSs from that source two of which are illustrated here in their yard a few months after acquisition. Unfortunately their condition was not good and a lot of refurbishment was required, nevertheless they gave Taylor's 5 years service and all went on to operate with subsequent owners. DMS 2141 awaits a repaint and DMS 2049 demonstrates the new order. **25 August 1988**

BOTTOM RIGHT: The third DMS acquired by Taylor's of Sutton Scotney was DM 1155 shown here in their depot receiving attention during the school summer holiday. **25 August 1988**

92

TOP LEFT: A very difficult vehicle to photograph was DM 1712 with Norman's coaches trading as Normenda Travels at Rowlands Castle. Seen here in their yard the bus still carries the name of its previous owner 'Norfolk Bluebird' on its side. **25 August 1988**

TOP RIGHT: Arrow Travel of Pulborough bought DM 1180 in 1982 and it was a highly reliable vehicle seen here in their yard. Some years later a deal with Haven bus would see it exchanged for DMS 2646. DM 1180 would end its days operating in New York. **25 August 1988**

CENTRE LEFT: In summer 1988 Ensignbus loaned DMS 192 to Fylde Borough Transport to operate an open top seafront service in Blackpool. It is seen here in front of RM 2071 at Blackpool Gynn Square. Note that the blind display advertises the time and day that the Regal Blue Devils were due to jump. **27 August 1988**

CENTRE RIGHT: Smith's Caoches of Shenington Ltd acquired a number of DMSs in a dealership capacity. Several operated for a short time until re-sale. However DMS 1896 entered service in the associated Smith's of Tysoe fleet. It is seen here in the Alcester yard with a white band added to its LT livery. **5 September 1988**

LEFT: How do you paint a bus? In this case DMS 1968 provides a demonstration in the yard of its new owner David Grasby at Oxhill. The painter was using the tractor bucket to raise himself to the upper deck level. The finished result appears later in this book. **5 September 1988**

93

ABOVE LEFT: Fred Pallett Catering bought two DMSs and use[d] them in their associated company Savoir Fare as mobile caterin[g] units. The second bus acquired was DMS 200 seen here at th[e] Nuneaton base. Note the reduced front entrance and panel ov[er] the lower windows. Normal loading and unloading was achieve[d] through the centre doors. This bus has long since disappeare[d] does it still exist?. **6 September 1988**

ABOVE: This bus, DMS 329 does still exist being with a priva[te] owner near Stafford. It is parked outside the office of Savoir Fare Nuneaton showing the reduction to the front door, but with low[er] windows retained. **6 September 1988**

LEFT: DMS 1835 had been acquired for conversion into a playbu[s] but following serious mechanical problems it was 'dumped' outsid[e] the factory of T B Precision at West Bromwich and used as [a] storeshed. **7 September 1988**

BELOW: Nellie The Elephant playbus DMS 1354 was picture[d] in service with West Midlands PTE in DMS ColourScen[e] 1979–1984. It was captured on film in Highgat[e] Birmingham. Like DMS 1613 pictured earlier this bus passed [to] New York Apple Tours as a static ticket office. **7 September 198[8]**

LEFT: DMS 831 passed from Midland Red North to Mrs Busby who used it to transport fruit pickers from Stafford to her farm and then around the site. Seen here on the farm. **9 September 1988**

LEFT: DMS 1460 would be withdrawn by Stevensons the following month having given two years service. Unusually the bus carries a blue livery with a Stevensons yellow lower front. **9 September 1988**

BELOW: The convertible open top DM 1220 in Stevensons dealer stock seen at Spath with their own DMS 241. DM 1220 would later see further service with Circle Line of Gloucester. **9 September 1988**

95

TOP LEFT: DMS 1584 was pictured in the first book with C Coaches in Cardiff, it then passed to Cottrell's Coaches Mitcheldean before entering the Stevensons fleet in spring 198 It is parked in the yard at Spath. **9 September 1988**

TOP RIGHT: This is DMS 1636 which was obtained as source of spare parts by Stevensons seen in the Spa yard. **9 September 1988**

ABOVE: Here is the finished result of the repaint by Dav Grasby of DMS 1968 at Oxhill. The application of black paint this manner is unusual. This was one of the DMSs fitted with Rolls Royce Eagle engine which it retained while with Grasb until sale. This bus still exists as a party bus albeit with a mo usual engine. Note also the former Green Line coach parke behind. **10 September 1988**

LEFT: DMS 2223 was acquired by Stevensons direct from L and operated for a couple of years. It was then re-sold Swanbrook Transport of Cheltenham and is pictured in the Staverton yard before the construction of their current mode office and workshop. This bus is still operational in Kent 2004. **10 September 1988**

LEFT: Circle Line of Gloucester would operate five DMSs and at some point most carried all over advertisements. DMS 2208 parked in their yard in the ornate livery for Cheltenham News / Gloucester Echo. **10 September 1988**

RIGHT: DMS 2129 seen with Mike DeCourcey Travel Ltd soon after acquisition from Graham's of Paisley and before repaint. The location is Coombe Abbey Country park Coventry. **11 September 1988**

LEFT : DMS 115 was one of the early DMSs with 'close together' headlights. It became a playbus with the Oxfordshire Playbus Association and was photographed at its new base, the Unipart car park in Cowley. This bus still exists in 2004 with a group based in Birkenhead. **12 September 1988**

97

LEFT: A return visit to Circle Line Gloucester was necessary to photograph some of their other DMSs. Here in the corner of their yard is DMS 1662 in 'Tesco' livery. **13 September 1988**

LEFT: To paint a bus pink takes some nerve, but the end result here on DMS 2187 in the Circle Line yard in Gloucester is rather stunning. This bus would become another example to serve as a static ticket office with New York Apple Tours. **13 September 1988**

BELOW LEFT: After service with WMPTE DMS 1319 was converted to become 'The Buzz' playbus in Coventry. Seen here after withdrawal at the Whitley Council depot. **14 September 1988**

BELOW: Rear view of DMS 1319 showing the rather crude upper deck emergency escape ladder. It is parked awaiting disposal in the Whitley Council depot next to a huge pile of rock salt. **14 September 1988**

LEFT: Trafalgar Square, London sees Cityrama DMS 2029 in part open top form and in an all over advertisement livery for BP. This bus would later operate tours in New York. **25 September 1988**

BELOW LEFT: Earlier in this book DM 982 was illustrated with Cream Line. Two years later and it is now in the Capitol Coaches of Cwmbran fleet. It is parked in Orchard Street Swansea. **1 October 1988**

BELOW: As mentioned earlier Lincoln City Transport bought four DMSs from Warrington. DMS 1484 with an appropriate Lincoln fleet number stands in the bus station on a grey October day. **15 October 1988**

LEFT: Ensignbus DMS 159 only carried this stunning livery for Saab for a very short time. It is parked in their Purfleet yard. **22 October 1988**

99

LEFT: The DMSs that had operated in the Southend Transport fleet returned to Ensignbus in autumn 1988. They initially operated on Ensignbus LRT services without repainting. Here DM 1008 stands in the Purfleet yard between duties complete with the Ensignbus fleetname applied to Southend livery. In 1991 this bus would be exported to Chicago for further operation. **22 October 1988**

RIGHT: This bus, DMS 353, has already appeared in this book twice in different liveries. It makes its third appearance in the extremely smart livery of Evan Evans Tours. Owned by Ensignbus it awaits customers at the Trocadero. **29 October 1988**

LEFT: A former Premier Travel Services DMS 1983 is pictured in the Ipswich buses yard as their No.99. The bus was acquired when Squirrell's Motor Services of Hitcham was taken over. Being non standard in the Ipswich fleet of atlanteans it was sold in mid 1989 into a non PSV role with CITB. It still exists in 2004 with at Enstone airfield. **30 December 1988**

North China – Jilin 1998
by Lennox MacEwan

Having heard that some DMSs had been exported direct from Manchester to "a northern Chinese city" I discovered that was Jilin and I was fortunate to be able to pay a short visit in 1998. Winter temperatures in this Province can drop to around -30°C with up to 40°C in the summer - not what the DMS was designed for or used to! Unfortunately, I was too late and I found only 3 DMSs working. Westerners are few and far between in Jilin and, whilst made welcome, I could not strike up any relationship with crews nor could I find anyone who could answer my queries (a major problem for an independent traveller) or help me locate the depot. So the visit simply recorded, I suspect, the latter days of the DMS in Jilin on route 30 working alongside Chinese built articulated single deckers. It is only speculation, but route 1 had recently received a fleet of brand new locally built 2 axle single deckers, all heavily used. Could it have been a DMS route? I doubt if we will ever know! *Lennox MacEwan*

ABOVE LEFT: Several B20 type DMSs that were formerly operated by Mybus of Manchester were exported to Jilin probably by Speedybus of Hong Kong. Jilin No. 6-505 is seen on an outbound journey. This is thought to be one of DMS 2494, 2497 or 2502. **14 November 1998**

LEFT: Ex-DM 2609, 6-503 seen under the trolleybus wires on an inbound journey in Jilin in somewhat bleak winter conditions. **14 November 1998**

BELOW: Now 6-505, one of the three former DMS type mentioned in the caption to the top photograph on this page, is seen outbound in Jilin. **14 November 1998**

LEFT: This is Jilin 6-505 which is probably one of the following: DMS 2494 or DMS 2497 or DMS 2502. **14 November 1998**

CENTRE LEFT: Now registered B3129? is Jilin 6-505 is seen working an outbound journey in Jilin. **14 November 1998**

BELOW: A front view of former DM 260? now 6-503 in the Jilin fleet. **14 November 1998**

BOTTOM LEFT: Jilin 6-506 is believed to be DMS 2342 seen working an outbound journey. **14 November 1998**

BOTTOM RIGHT: This is probably DMS 234? now registered B31663 and numbered 6-506 in Jilin seen here on an outbound journey. **14 November 1998**

North China – Dalian 1997–2001
by Lennox MacEwan

Dalian is a large seaport in Liaoning Provice known as the Hong Kong of the north. It doesn't quite have a Hong Kong climate with winter temperatures down to -10°C, but summer is quite up to Hong Kong standards. The Tong Da Bus Company ran a fleet of former British double deckers, all arriving via use in Hong Kong, and this included 8 or so DMSs. They all operated on route 401 from the city centre out to the seaside, terminating at the Sea Horizon Hotel. The depot was on the route and all the buses appeared to have their own crews with all breaks/shift changes taken by running empty to/from the Sea Horizon Hotel terminus. The fleet was popular with the staff and was well looked after - the cleaning of the buses being a crew duty with internal cleaning taking place en route and washing the exterior at the start or end of the shift. In the 90s, most vehicles were in all over advertising livery but latterly, the majority was simply turned out in fleet livery of yellow with a red skirt. All good things must come to an end and that came in April 2001 when all were replaced by 2-axle single deckers of Chinese manufacture. During the 1990s, up to 6 DMSs could be seen in service, but in March 2001, only 2 were in service namely 02 and 04; another four were out of use forming a wind shelter at the depot servicing pit and the other 2 had been driven off to a destination unknown accompanied by 6 of the other former KMB Fleetlines. Sad indeed, but predictable.
Lennox MacEwan

TOP: Former LT and CMB DM 1189 is seen on an outbound journey at Jie Fang Lu. Now number 08 with Tong DA Bus Company. **5 November 1997**

CENTRE LEFT: Former LT and CMB DM 1205 seen at Jie Fang Lu in an all over advertisement livery for 888, while working as Tong DA Bus Company No. 04, Speedy Bus logos were also carried. **5 November 1997**

CENTRE RIGHT: Carrying the same advertisement livery as DM 1205 is former DM 1204 now Tong DA Bus Company 05 seen outbound at Jie Fang Lu, note the Speedy Bus logos.
5 November 1997

BOTTOM: A third vehicle in advert livery for 888 and with Speedy Bus logos is former DM 1202 now Tong DA Bus Company 07 also seen outbound at Jie Fang Lu. **5 November 1997**

103

TOP: Carrying registration B93649 is Tong DA Bus Company No.2 now in this all over advertisement livery at Jie Fang Lu. This bus was originally DM 929 and XF132 in the CMB fleet. **5 November 1997**

CENTRE RIGHT: Tong DA Bus Company 06 is former DM 1206 seen at Jie Fang Lu carrying an all over advertisement livery for Jia Mai. **5 November 1997**

BELOW RIGHT: This is DM 1189 and now number 08 in the Tong DA Bus Company fleet. It is seen at Jie Fang Lu. **5 November 1997**

LEFT: This is former DM 929 now Tong DA Bus Company 02, it is seen inbound between the Sea Horizon Hotel and the depot advertising bottled water.
11 November 1998

BELOW: Former DM 1205 advertising bottled water is seen at the depot stop at Fujia Zhuang on an outbound working with Tong DA Bus Company in whose fleet it has become 04.
11 November 1998

BOTTOM: Tong DA Bus Company 01 was originally DMS 865 seen here carrying an advertisement for Jia Mei near the depot at Fujia Zhuang.
11 November 1998

RIGHT: Tong DA Bus Company No.01 is ex CMB XF 130 originally DMS 865 seen here in Dalian outbound near the depot, carrying an all over advertisement for Jia Mei Ao. **6 November 1997**

RIGHT: DM 1189 speeds along in Dalian as Tong DA Bus Company No. 08. **5 November 1997**

BELOW: Tong DA Bus Company No. 06 was formerly CMB XF 167 and originally DM 1206 seen en route between the Sea Horizon Hotel and the depot. **11 November 1998**

ABOVE: Various former Hong Kong vehicles line up in the depot of Tong DA Bus Company in Dalian including No. 07 originally DM1202, which was pictured with CMB in DMS ColourScene Hong Kong, and 04 which was DM 1205. **11 November 1998**

LEFT: Seen outbound at Jie Fang Lu is Tong DA Bus Company 06. This was originally DM 1206. **13 November 1998**

BELOW: DM 1202 was previously XF170 in the CMB fleet. Now 07 in the Tong DA Bus Company fleet it is seen at Jie Fang Lu. **13 November 1998**

107

LEFT: Tong DA Bus Company 07 was origina[lly] DM 1202 is seen near the depot on an inbou[nd] journey in Dalian. **4 April 2000**

BELOW: Looking extremely smart is Tong D[A] Bus Company No. 03, this is DM 1208 previous[ly] CMB XF 163, it is outbound on route 401 a[t] Jie Fang Lu. **7 April 2000**

BOTTOM LEFT: This is the standard fleet live[ry] of Tong DA Bus Company, fleet number 06, D[M] 1206 seen approaching the Sea Horizon Hotel [in] Dalian. **4 April 2000**

BOTTOM RIGHT: UK offside view of Tong D[A] Bus Company 06, DM 1206 showing th[e] repositioned entrance doors inbound at the Se[a] Horizons Hotel in Dalian. **4 April 2000**

108

LEFT: DM 1202 now Tong DA Bus Company No.07 has been repainted since the earlier view, it is approaching the Sea Horizon Hotel in Dalian. **4 April 2000**

CENTRE LEFT: DM 1206 is seen in Dalian between the Sea Horizon Hotel terminus and the depot, now numbered 06 and formerly CMB XF 167. **4 April 2000**

BELOW LEFT: Carrying Tong DA Bus Company fleet livery is 01 seen working an inbound journey between the sea Horizon Hotel and the depot. This bus was originally DMS 865. **4 April 2000**

BELOW RIGHT: DM 1205 is now 04 and registered B93669 in the Dalian Tong DA Bus Company fleet seen here inbound between the Sea Horizon Hotel terminus and the depot. **4 April 2000**

109

LEFT: Tong DA bus Company 03 formerly CMB XF 163 and origina[l] DM 1208 is seen in Dalian on a[n] inbound journey near Sea Horiz[on] terminus. **4 April 2000**

CENTRE LEFT: Tong DA B[us] Company 06 was originally DM 12[0?] seen here at the City Terminu[s] **6 April 2000**

CENTRE RIGHT: DM 1205 is no[w] Tong DA Bus Company 04, it is work between the Sea Horizon Ho[tel] terminus and the depot. **6 April 20[00]**

BOTTOM: Tong DA Bus Compan[y] 03 now registered B93667 and wa[s] originally DM 1208 it is picture[d] between the Sea Horizon hotel a[nd] the depot. **6 April 2000**

LEFT: Tong DA Bus Company No. 04 in fleet livery is former CMB XF 165 originally DM 1205 at the Sea Horizons Hotel terminus. **2 March 2001**

BELOW: Tong DA Bus Company No. 02 originally DM 929 and previously CMB XF 132 seen in fleet livery picking up passengers at the City Terminus on Qing Nie Jie. **2 March 2001**

BOTTOM: Two DMSs at the Sea Horizons Hotel terminus with the Tong DA Bus Company on the left is 02, DM 929 and next to it is 04, DM 1205 both in fleet livery. Note the different entrance doors; a CMB modification. These were the last two DMSs in use in Dalian. **2 March 2001**

111

DMS ColourScene Vol 3 - Index.

Buses are indexed by London Transport fleet number, followed by the date on which that bus was photographed, each caption showing the date for easy reference. Photos are arranged in date order within their sections with some minor exceptions in the China pages.

DMS/DM Class no.	Date of photograph(s)
United Kingdom	
24	18.05.86
36	06.07.85
64	18.05.86
112	18.05.86
115	12.09.88
136	06.10.85
	25.10.87
158	18.05.86
159	22.10.88
165	26.07.86
188	28.09.86 F
192	25.05.86
	27.08.88
200	06.09.88
210	31.05.86
237	02.09.85
241	09.09.88
264	11.08.85
270	01.06.86
276	27.09.87
287	18.05.86
290	09.03.85
294	19.06.86
	21.08.88
299	23.08.87
315	25.05.86
325	25.05.86
326	27.08.86
329	06.09.88
343	06.07.85
353	25.05.86
	09.07.88 x 2
	29.10.88
358	28.08.86
392	31.01.87
	24.01.88
415	12.07.86
416	07.09.85
434	14.06.86
439	01.07.86
440	23.07.88
461	24.06.88
464	16.07.88
466	13.08.88
550	20.07.86
	25.10.86
553	23.07.88
558	19.04.88
559	07.09.85
582	01.06.86
589	21.04.85
590	12.08.85
	02.09.85
648	30.01.88
661	05.09.86
664	09.07.87
665	20.04.88
668	19.04.88
672	13.09.86
679	13.09.86
702	15.08.87
768	25.06.88
806	22.05.87
821	29.08.86
831	09.09.88
852	18.05.86 x 2
	25.05.87
	07.05.88
853	18.05.86
860	29.08.86
867	18.05.86
886	22.06.85
892	01.06.86
930	21.06.87
939	18.05.86
958	05.04.86
962	28.05.88
964	18.05.86
979	23.05.87
982	02.08.86
	01.10.88
995	22.05.87
	23.07.87
999	09.07.87
1001	04.05.86
1003	14.06.86
1008	22.10.88
1019	06.10.85
1020	06.05.85
1022	02.08.86
1023	14.06.86
1051	03.08.85
1052	02.08.86
1059	18.05.86
1067	14.06.86
	28.11.87 RC
1069	06.05.85

DMS/DM Class no.	Date of photograph(s)
1074	18.05.86
1081	10.09.87
1086	25.06.88
1090	23.07.87
1097	12.07.86
1101	21.03.87
1102	25.05.87
1106	24.05.85
1108	22.07.87
1110	25.05.86
1117	21.06.87
1121	22.06.85
1129	18.05.86
1132	18.05.86
1134	18.05.86
1137	25.06.88
1138	05.09.86
1146	25.10.87
	16.01.88
1154	18.05.86
1155	25.08.88
1159	03.07.88
1166	18.05.86
1170	18.05.86
1178	23.05.86
1180	25.08.88
1181	25.06.88
1217	14.06.86
1219	29.08.86
1220	14.09.86
	09.09.88
1237	14.09.85
1240	23.05.86
1245	22.06.85
1256	26.05.86
1258	08.06.85
1263	07.09.85
1283	28.09.85
1287	01.06.86
1290	12.07.87
1298	07.09.85
1308	06.06.87
1318	01.06.86
1319	14.09.88 x 2
1348	26.07.86
1354	07.09.88
1358	01.06.86
	02.01.87
1361	01.06.86
1371	26.07.86
1377	01.06.86
1402	23.07.87
1427	09.08.86
1440	21.04.88
1441	22.04.88
1444	21.03.87
1449	02.06.85
1451	19.04.88
1460	09.09.88
1468	07.09.85
1469	25.10.87
	19.04.88 x 2
1484	15.10.88
1487	13.07.85 FC
1490	28.11.87
1502	13.09.86
1503	13.07.85 FC
1504	13.07.85
1509	16.04.88
1512	25.04.87
1516	20.09.86
	25.04.87
1526	13.09.86
	25.04.87
1528	25.04.87
	22.04.88
1543	21.07.87
1548	11.10.86
1552	28.09.85
	13.08.88
1584	09.09.88
1604	12.05.85
1611	21.11.87
1613	05.09.86
1614	30.01.88
1616	04.07.87
1636	09.09.88
1645	28.11.87
1647	29.08.86
1649	16.01.88
1650	21.11.87
1652	15.01.88
1655	14.06.86
1659	28.11.87
1662	13.09.88
1667	06.06.87
1673	21.06.87
1681	16.07.88

DMS/DM Class no.	Date of photograph(s)
1682	21.04.85
	04.05.86
1689	20.09.86
1695	16.04.88
1703	16.04.88
1705	01.06.86
1706	17.08.85
1707	12.07.86
1709	03.08.86
1710	25.10.87
1712	25.08.88
1713	19.04.88
	21.04.88
1715	16.06.85
1721	19.05.85
1726	01.07.86
1728	17.08.85
1738	18.05.86
1758	18.05.86
1797	19.05.85
	07.06.86
1800	14.05.88
	21.05.88
1802	14.09.85
1803	19.05.85
1827	23.05.87
1830	01.06.85
	16.05.87
1831	27.03.86
1834	25.05.86
1835	07.09.88
1842	27.05.88
1843	13.04.86
1844	21.03.87
1847	15.04.88
1849	17.08.85
1854	04.10.87
1880	29.08.87
1881	12.07.86
1893	17.08.85
1894	15.04.88
1896	05.09.88
1898	18.05.86
	10.08.86
1911	20.07.87
1915	16.04.88
1917	15.04.88
1923	18.05.86
	07.05.88
1924	14.09.85 x 2
	09.04.88
1942	20.07.87
1943	08.09.87
	21.05.88
1944	10.05.87
1948	17.08.85
1949	24.05.85
1951	23.05.86
1962	21.07.87
1968	05.09.88
	10.09.88
1973	20.09.86
1981	09.07.87
1983	07.06.86
	30.05.87
	30.12.88
1984	02.08.86
1986	16.04.88
1988	05.06.88 x 2
1989	30.05.87
1991	07.06.87 x 2
2000	13.08.85
2001	03.07.86
2005	01.06.86
	12.06.88
2019	07.06.87
2023	05.04.86 x 2
	09.07.88
2024	12.07.86
2025	27.06.87
2026	23.05.86
2027	21.11.87
2028	27.06.87
2029	25.09.88
2030	14.07.87
2031	21.11.87
2033	11.10.86
2034	25.04.87
2035	27.06.87
2037	20.04.88
2038	25.10.87
2041	24.08.85
	14.04.88
2043	3.08.88
2046	20.04.88
2049	25.08.88
2051	13.08.88
2056	10.08.86
2057	19.04.88

DMS/DM Class no.	Date of photograph(s)
2069	25.05.85 F
2082	25.06.88
2089	17.08.85
2094	16.07.88
2095	25.06.88
2120	23.05.87
2125	25.10.87
2129	11.09.88
2131	27.06.87
2137	19.04.88
2141	25.08.88
2148	12.08.85
2152	16.07.88
2161	19.04.88
2164	13.03.88
2167	18.05.86
2169	14.04.88 F
2170	14.04.88 F
2174	24.08.85
	14.04.88
2175	14.04.88
2182	13.08.88
2187	13.09.88
2192	07.06.86
2195	07.06.87
2203	14.04.88
2208	10.09.88
2214	20.04.88
2216	10.05.86
2221	10.05.86
2222	07.11.87
2223	10.09.88
2224	14.04.88 F
2226	19.07.86
	06.09.87 RC
2227	24.08.85
2232	16.07.88
2238	07.12.87
2239	06.07.85
2243	10.08.86
	13.03.88
SYPTE 1526	21.03.87
SYPTE 1529	29.03.87
USA – Denver	
147	14.10.91
180	14.10.91
185	14.10.91 x 2
211	14.10.91
232	14.10.91 x 2
283	14.10.91 x 3 RC
304	14.10.91 x 3 RC
312	14.10.91
340	14.10.91
363	14.10.91 x 3
USA – Chicago	
729	21.10.91
926	21.10.91
939	21.10.91
1037	22.10.91
	23.10.91 x 2
1072	21.10.91
1101	21.10.91
1113	21.10.91
1157	23.10.91
1701	23.10.91
1710	20.10.91 x 2
	22.10.91
1949	21.10.91
USA – New York	
372	04.10.94
719	02.10.94 RC
935	04.10.94
953	30.09.94
1004	01.10.94
	04.10.94
1015	01.10.94
	04.10.94
1118	03.10.94
	04.10.94
1447	04.10.94
1720	01.10.94
1836	04.10.94
1839	30.09.94
1873	01.10.94
	04.10.94
1977	30.09.94
1982	01.10.94
1984	01.10.94
	04.10.94
2101	04.10.94
2119	04.10.94
2182	04.10.94
2188	04.10.94
2407	04.10.94
SYPTE 1510	30.09.94

DMS/DM Class no.	Date of photograph(s)
Hong Kong	
167	02.05.92
184	30.04.92
240	09.11.90
316	09.05.92
479	09.11.90
557	28.04.92
605	27.04.94
638	09.05.92
663	13.03.81
765	11.11.95
788	??.02.83
794	28.04.92
796	??.09.81
798	??.09.81
835	11.11.95
891	09.05.92
894	26.04.92
902	01.05.92
911	03.05.92
916	09.11.90
927	11.11.95
929	03.05.92
983	15.11.90
992	10.11.90
1053	01.05.92
1084	??.09.81
1085	??.07.81
	??.09.81
	24.04.92
1187	10.11.90
1198	10.11.90
1551	28.04.92
1554	28.04.92 x 2
1759	??.07.81
2092	10.11.90
2144	03.05.92
2145	30.04.92
2150	14.04.83
	??.??.84
2160	02.05.92
2374	11.11.95
2426	27.04.94
2466	11.11.95
MD66	30.04.92
South China – Guangzhou	
142	10.05.93 x 2
1745	26.04.94 x 3
2130	26.04.94
2149	10.05.93
2165	26.04.94 x 2
2178	10.05.93 x 2
2207	26.04.94
NK	26.04.94 x 2
North China – Dalian	
865	06.11.97
	11.11.98
	04.04.00
929	05.11.97
	11.11.98
	02.03.01 x 2
1189	05.11.97 x 3
1202	05.11.97
	11.11.98
	13.11.98
	04.04.00 x 2
1204	05.11.97
1205	05.11.97
	11.11.98
	04.04.00
	06.04.00
	02.03.01 x 2
1206	05.11.97
	11.11.98 x 2
	13.11.98
	04.04.00 x 3
	06.04.00
1208	04.04.00
	06.04.00
	07.04.00
North China – Jilin	
2342	14.11.98 x 2
NK (2494/2497/2502)	14.11.98 x 4
2609	14.11.98 x 3 R(

NOTES:
FC – Front Cover
RC – Rear Cover
F – Frontispiece / Foreword

112